I0163388

In Search of Ruth or Boaz

It's not just about religion

By Sue Thomas

In Search of Ruth or Boaz

It's Not Just About Religion

By Sue Thomas

Illustrated by

Lauren Jones

In Search of Ruth or Boaz

Also, by Sue Thomas:

A Three-Ring Circus

I Forgot to Forgive Myself

In Search of Ruth or Boaz

Printed in the United States of America

Library of Congress No: 1-13368297621

by Sue Thomas

Illustrated by Lauren Jones

DEDICATION

For my children, Super Dave and Awesome Matt,

Thank you, Father God, for honoring me to become a mom. Thank you, Jesus, for guiding me, and helping me raise my sons, may the Holy Spirit forever cover, protect, order your steps, and burn a fire in your heart for God. I am blessed to have given birth to you both. Thank you both for being strong, independent, and standing firm against all odds. Most of all thank you for being the best sons. I love you both. My dear sons, may God continue in his promise to shower you with all the blessings he chooses to bestow upon you and yours. I ask God to bless both of you seven generations forward, as each of your children and their children do the same in the Lord. One of my humble prayers has always been for God to bless my children and my children's children.

* * * * * * * * * * * * * * * * * *

ACKNOWLEDGMENT

To God in Heaven, thank you for holding me up and leading me in the proper direction. Thank you for knowing beforehand not only the valleys, mountains, and hills in which you would accompany me and walk alongside me, but also the gutters of murk you would rescue me from. Thank you for using me, even when I did not want to be used. To my children, grandson, and future grandchildren, you are loved. Always remember that my love for you is infinite!

To my siblings, we are one of an eternal bond that has intertwined us forever through our mom, Odette, who instilled her love in our veins. We support and love one another because of her, and we are passing the love on to the next generation, as well as others.

To Antoine Nicolas, William and Jason, although you contributed to my books in different ways, please know that your help in my writing projects was a Godsend and is immensely appreciated. I got the love bug of writing.

To my nieces, nephews, grandnieces, grandnephews, cousins, and host of extended family of in-laws, may we continue to bond and connect through many generations to come. May God continue to bless us, as he connects us to our ancestors to light our path to a brighter future.

In Search of Ruth or Boaz

To my friends, associates, co-workers, and neighbors' thanks for your kind words, when I needed them. I appreciate you supporting me throughout my journey, especially when I felt I was at my lowest, thank you!

To the outstanding and influential scholars in my life, thank you for educating me correctly so I may educate and elevate others. To the incredible women who will take on the role of Ruth in my children's lives, I am entrusting you with the care of my sons and our future generations to come.

To my fellow nurses, although underpaid and undervalued, know that you are the backbone of the nursing industry. Keep giving your best. Our patients deserve it. Go Knights! Charge on!

To the sweet and kind-hearted man who will become my Boaz, I understand that dealing with me is no small task. I know that you will rise to the occasion because I am worthy!

Thank you to my followers on social media for your support.

* * * * * * * * * * * * * * * * * * *

IN MEMORIAM

To the memory of my mom, Odette Rospide & my eldest sister, Zita Milfort, you both are forever in my heart. You will not be forgotten. May you both forever rest in peace!

* * * * * * * * * * * * * * * * * * *

DISCLAIMER

This work is the result of the author's personal experience and vivid imagination, and it has taken the direction that was intended. The writer's goal was to explore single, married, the influences of matchmaking and the personal choice made by an individual. Please note that the author should not be held responsible for any perceived likeness, self-descriptive similarities, possible triggers, or character portrayals in this book. The author does not assume any responsibility for any coincidental interpretations or misinterpretations. You are the author of your own life's story. This work represents a personal perspective and perception of the author and may include references to certain Biblical verses based on opinions. It is not the intention of the author to offend any reader, their cultural or religious beliefs, nor have anyone offend mine. If for any reason you feel differently, it is recommended to either give the book away or choose not to read it. Please note that this book is intended for peaceful, thought-provoking discussions and does not serve as a self-help or guidebook on relationships. Additionally, this book should not be considered blasphemy. The content of the book is meant for adult readers and may contain adult language. This book or its contents may not be reformatted. Adult Content

* * * * * * * * * * * * * * * * * * *

PRAYER THROUGH VERSES

Psalms 27 The LORD is my light and my salvation; Whom shall I fear? The LORD is the strength of my life; Of whom shall I be afraid? 2 When the wicked came against me to eat up my flesh, my enemies and foes, they stumbled and fell. 3 Though an army may encamp against me, my heart shall not fear; Though war may rise against me, in this I will be confident. 4 One thing I have desired of the LORD, that will I seek: That I may dwell in the house of the LORD All the days of my life, to behold the beauty of the Lord, and to inquire in His temple.

* * * * * * * * * * * * * * * * * * *

Lamentations 3: 25-26 The Lord is good to those who wait for Him, to the soul who seeks Him. 26 It is good that one should hope and wait quietly for the salvation of the Lord.

* * * * * * * * * * * * * * * * * * *

Psalms 23: The LORD is my shepherd; I shall not want. 2 He makes me to lie down in green pastures; He leads me beside the still waters. 3 He restores my soul; He leads me in the paths of righteousness For His name's sake. 4 Yea, though I walk through the valley of the shadow of death, I will fear no evil; For You are with me; Your rod and Your staff, they comfort me. 5 You prepare a table before me in the presence of my enemies; You anoint my head with oil; My cup runs over. 6 Surely goodness and mercy shall follow me All the days of my life; And I will dwell in the house of the LORD Forever.

* * * * * * * * * * * * * * * * * * *

Galatians 9: 6 And let us not grow weary while doing good, for in due season we shall reap if we do not lose heart. 10 Therefore, as we have opportunity, let us do good to all, especially to those who are of the household of faith. (NKJV)

* * * * * * * * * * * * * * * * * * *

2 Chronicles 7: 14 If My people who are called by My name will humble themselves, and pray and seek My face, and turn from their wicked ways, then I will hear from heaven, and will forgive their sin and heal their land. (NKJV)

* * * * * * * * * * * * * * * * * * *

Joshua 24:15 "...But as for me and my house, we will serve the Lord". (NKJV)

* * * * * * * * * * * * * * * * * * *

1 Corinthians 13:4 "Love suffers long and is kind; love does not envy; love does not parade itself, is not puffed up; 5 does not behave rudely, does not seek its own, is not provoked, thinks no evil; 6 does not rejoice in

iniquity, but rejoices in the truth; 7 bears all things, believes all things, hopes all things, endures all things".

* * * * * * * * * * * * * * * * * * *

CONTENTS

INTRODUCTION

The intricacies of relationships, marriage, dating, and matchmaking in today's society can be quite different from the story of Ruth.

As I delved into the subject, my thoughts flowed like the Nile River, and I was exploring the various aspects and their complexities. I realized that not everyone may be familiar with the biblical story. As part of the discussion of relationships, it is important to provide a summary of Ruth's journey in finding Boaz, her life partner because there are so many elements that connect us to the era of Ruth and Boaz, which still applies today.

One of the things that has also needed to be made clear is that in the olden days, men were placed in charge of everything, including the head of the church, businesses, and households. Although women mostly reared children, men were in charge and consequently set the rules. There were roles that men were assigned according to the tribes or clans in terms of inheritance. While in certain instances things have not departed that drastically from then, and most women within that hierarchy were considered as property, women showed greatness even in the background.

Ruth is depicted as an exemplary woman. Ruth was also hard-working and independent. While Boaz was a genuinely remarkable man of great means, he remained humble. They are indeed an ideal package, both separately and together. They are a great match when it comes to describing attributes that are appealing in finding a partner. However, if it were not for Ruth's mother-in-law, Naomi, the quintessential example of a matchmaker, Ruth and Boaz dating may have been slim to none. Traditional and cultural values of matchmaking still take place today; so much so that when individuals actively search for a companion to share their lives with, they hope to find someone like Ruth or Boaz who will reciprocate love, marry, offer care, support financially, engage in intimate relations, and start a family. I am not embarking on a romance novel or fairytale where we find ourselves gushing, dreaming, fantasizing, and wishing.

We are not looking for a charming prince or princess charming. Rather, I would like to engage in captivating conversations about individual choices that may potentially redirect our paths in life's journey. Love can be romanticized depending on the lenses viewing it. Also, matchmaking on a subpar level still exists, as we are influenced by so many factors. We ask family, and friends if their friend has a friend, and our parents ask their friends at work or church if they know a nice man or young lady. In addition, do not forget the various dating apps, we get offers from our friends, saying, "do you want me to set you up?" There are, however, various forms of matchmaking. Matchmaking has been around for centuries, and it will continue to eternity.

Relationships are complex enough and may not need a boost or nudge from anyone. Nevertheless, as parents, we pray for God to find our children a partner. When this does not happen soon enough, we play matchmaker. While certain folks prefer to remain single, there are also those who prefer to make their own choices in finding love. Knowing that there are plenty of fish in the sea, we mingle, have coffee with bagel, and remain in harmony in different book clubs, social groups and church groups, bumble, fumble, but we will not become unhinged, and our tender connections when we sit around in self-thought of our match with Cupid, the question becomes – Are we in love? And if so, is this what we want?

A relationship is bigger than a matchmaker's dream, however choosy or rebellious its intended culprits. Love is an action word; we must make it do something. We wonder, who will our partners be? The choice is endless as there are billions of us to choose from. Once we decide that the first pick is who we want to be with, we cannot sit idly by and expect a match to happen on its own out of thin air. We pray and hope that this works out for us. However, only God may show us better than He can tell us because we do not listen well. He allows us the choice to rebel and deviate from whomever. God will allow us to go down that road, and He will walk right alongside us.

The same steps we choose to take in our journey as we place one foot in front the other, are the ones that are going to be putting our life's puzzle together. Yes, each step is a choice. School, career, marriage, children, infidelity, even happiness as opposed to sadness, is a choice. We must realize every choice is an act of war because nothing worth fighting for comes easily. Not everyone wants to defend themselves. Instead of having disagreements in keeping the peace, we would rather go along to get along. Do you feel like you have to explain your decision?

Defiance. Authenticity. Truth. Yes. No. Love. Guidance. Self-love. Peace. Sacrifice. I do. Match. It all boils down to one thing, choice!

* * * * * * * * * * * * * * * * * * *

Chapter I

A Human Touch

There was a period a few years ago, where dating, matchmaking, even weddings took a backseat on a social scale. The Pandemic lockdown was stressful for those who were in the dating pool. Despite the slowdown of physical contact due to the pandemic, the desire to date and meet new people went idled, however, despite health concerns, individuals found a way to connect. Certain protocols were put in place, which deferred, but did not prevent many hangouts from taking place. Even though folks continued to face challenges in finding a romantic partner, they still met at internet cafés, parks, etc., with their masks and all. This to me says it all, that love will find a way, as exemplified by Ruth and Boaz.

Oddly enough, during this global crisis, it did seem contradictory to maintain a six-feet social distance in the airport line, only to be crammed on the plane with all those people. If anything, the pandemic has emphasized the importance of human connection, which is as certain, and anticipated as the break of dawn's early light. It's as astounding as a receding sunset. It is as natural as Niagara Falls' mists. Moreover, it is the ebb and flow of the high and low tides. Additionally, it is the yin and yang of life. Understanding these concepts signifies the balance, harmony, and progress of nature, which is the essence of our world.

When we resist that force of nature, chaos may ensue. Should the need for love and the insatiable longing to belong fail, this level of Maslow's hierarchy of needs would become non-existent. It also begs the question, why do we deceive ourselves and proceed to deceive others, as well, about how innocent and pure we are? Many of us place ourselves so high on the mantle, that we may feel holier than thou. Saints, spiritual awareness is to acknowledge and remember that in the Western world, some of the hems of our garments were once way above our knees. We used to dance and dress provocatively at nightclubs and were promiscuous. Many of us forget to ask ourselves, did we not feel passion at least once in our lifetime? Is it not ok to have feelings? Are we just stoically going through life, lifeless? Were we conceived through immaculate conception? Only Christ was. We are not pure. It's almost as if blood does not run through our veins or we have no tingling feelings or sensation when a mere glance or someone of interest's hand brushes against our skin sends our spider-sense awry. Romans

3:23 "For all have sinned and fall short of the glory of God".

We have forgotten that we were once youthful. The irony is although we desire human contact, our regard is stifled, as we thumb our noses on what was once our lives. On the other hand, dating with the advent of social media has given us so many options, that we are so hurried to disconnect or delete one another from our hearts, that we do not revel or enjoy in the present and the now of Maslow's need. I am not just saying fight for the simple pleasures because it may be against your upbringing. However, I am referring to recognition of the awareness deficit span in having multiple or simultaneous interests and not directing our thoughts to one person. Oftentimes, this may cause confusion for others who are seeking your undivided attention. We enjoy being the center of scrutiny on a media app with the click of the "Like" "Follow" or "Comments" buttons blinking into the thousands; but may still feel lonely because the next text or post seems more important than what is currently going on. It keeps us disconnected to a conversation with a date because there are mixed signals. Yes, phones and social media keep us busy with each ping sound.

The longing for contact may still be there for sentimental attachment. However, the connection may not happen because of the curiosity of a pre-planned match, another new viewer and numerous "likes" from an app. Today, we live in a society where individuals are in a rush to swipe left in a social or dating app construct. But we are so quick to erase, discard, ignore, or shelf others for later use in a date or potential date that we do not realize we have given up on our well-being in remaining attached to a good partner. Furthermore, we turn down the kindness of someone who should continue to be an integral part of our hearts. Because they are not flamboyant, outlandish, and may be found boring, we terminate contact. In most relationships, the connection is there. However, the link demands that the fires to establish or rekindle a relationship endure. Albeit, our spontaneous resilience may be understated, but we navigate and keep pushing through the channels to stand united.

Imagine a life likened to the initial opening of COVID. Similarly to the 1980s where fear of the AIDS epidemic and its unknown cure sent folks into panic mode because so many folks were dying, COVID, too, brought death and despair. The shared unpredictability kept the population on edge. You know, lockdown, social distancing, few human interactions, masks, gloves, border closings, or brief contact with the realm at large. Due to the epidemic, companies changed their business models to allow their employees to work from home. Individuals ordered takeout and deliveries which were dropped off by the front doors. A person could not visit a loved one at the hospital or nursing home facilities often, even after receiving multiple Covid vaccinations. For the risk that Covid would spread, and the Pandemic would continue to thrive, some individuals would allow no one in their house for fear of having COVID and passing away. There were awkward traveling scenarios, being outdoors without a facial contraption, which prevented people from having excess conversation with each other at close range, and less handholding.

At the height of what they dubbed as "social distancing" certain individuals would rather not chance meeting someone new and having intimate contact unless they wanted to chance death from the possibility of attaining COVID. During the Pandemic some folks worked from home or followed hybrid work models. Countries faced death and despair in the lockdown but collaborated with advances made in medicine. There were numerous vaccines and new CDC rules implemented in the United States. As impactful as it was with all that was happening, babies continued to be born.

Facing the uncertainties of the pandemic may have appeared cold and drab, but we not only satisfied the needs of humanity, but we also shared the fear of the unknown, intimacy prevailed, and we got through the pandemic! So, what was the result? One thing in social science we learned is that we have much more to learn. The pandemic, which was an epic-world-wide horrible period, affecting millions of families, hundreds of thousands of deaths, billions in costs, and countries closing their borders, has taught us nothing, as a society and as human beings. Unity went right back to selfishness and individualism.

Post-pandemic, marriage venues reopened, churches, clubs, bars, bingo halls, sorority, and dance halls, among other venues, were full again. Matchmaking relatives had returned to attempt pairing, and the ads of dating apps were back in full throttle and opened for business. Dating apps are supposed to connect people, while saving potential clients time, as well as alleviating the desperation and anxiety of finding a mate. The more apps one uses, the higher the chances of matching with a compatible person and finding Ruth or Boaz.

Pairing two-by-two is not a new concept. In the first book of the Holy Bible, God may have considered this necessary because every other animal had a mate, so God determined Adam should have one too. Before the flood, people had been paired off with a partner by the elders, in this effort, relatives will continue this for centuries to come. Genesis 6:19 "And of every living thing of all flesh you shall bring two of every sort into the ark, to keep them alive with you; they shall be male and female. 20 Of the birds after their kind, of animals after their kind, and of every creeping thing of the earth after its kind, two of every kind will come to you to keep them alive".

Since then, generations have been assigned a partner by family members, friends, and well-wishers. Many of those who were matched have survived. I did not say that all these unions would be great and tied into a nice bow and everyone would live happily ever after. I am reflecting on how folks are matched or paired off, whether they want to be. Some of us do not get to choose!

As a woman, I have observed that marriage may not just be a choice between two people getting together to agree on a covenant. Additionally, I have noticed that certain ethnic or religious individuals may not give women the option to reject a partner whom they do not even like, much less be attached to, for an eternity. Worse, they may have planned that partnership for them since birth! When caregivers have gone to great lengths, how can one refuse such an offer? Our parents mean well and want better for us, right?

In most arranged marriages, there is nothing for the illustrious bride to do as hundreds of invited guests, friends, and extended family are present and they just have to appear for the ceremony and utter, "I do"! A pastor, justice of the peace, or notary public can marry the couple. These observances may be extravagant, or we may hold them in the kitchen or the backyard. When two people want to be together, they should form that union, as they see fit. The events have even become a hoity-toity, or fanciful functions sometimes, whereby the group may be compensated with a dowry that will benefit the household. Oh, yes, Ma'am Pam, and likewise one upper, meaning outdoing a relative or friend's nuptials by having the rites for your occasion performed in a castle in the Caribbean, because your friend had a major celebration on the beaches in Italy. Nine times out of ten, when many of these people return to the real world, their bank accounts are overdrawn, and they cannot afford the rent of a one-bedroom apartment. But the celebrity-like wedding ceremony was a success, as they made continuous mortgage payments to the venue until the ceremony was paid off years later. Could you have afforded a destination wedding? Go Figure!

In other instances, the fantasy of a marriage is seeing a dream becoming reality. The picturesque setting of wearing an expensive flowing wedding gown, a veil, and a long silky-laced-train is a lot like a little prince or princess' dream come true, depending on who is dreaming. We desire to reconnect and go on love's plateau! "What's love got to do with it"? It depends! Are we putting more emphasis on a ceremony, or should we concentrate on what is to come in a lifelong marriage?

There is a difference, as a wedding is a celebratory ceremony lasting a day, and a marriage is a formal, legal binding union between two individuals recognized by a state or country that is supposed to last a lifetime. It is a partnership with another individual to commune with, kiss, make love to, snuggle, struggle, wake up next to, and have a family with, or whatever that may entail.

Before you take that leap into a serious relationship, a person should ask themselves, "Are we friends?" Before anything, this is one of the most significant questions you will ask because in the beginning there was friendship, followed by dating, engagement, then marriage, etc. Ask yourself again, "Do you love them, or did you just get comfortable and now feel stuck?" In other words, is this person the desire of your heart? Psalms 37:4 "Delight yourself also in the Lord, And He shall give you the desires of your heart". Stop and think about it.

As life progresses, are you still friends or do you feel there is nothing left to sustain the marriage? Well, individuals seeking a life partner must navigate their own path in finding the right match. An individual in search of Ruth, the biblical character depicted as a virtuous woman, is the epitome of what one may wish for in a wife. Proverbs 18:22, "He who finds a wife finds a good thing, and obtains favor from the Lord". Boaz on the other hand, is a gentleman who exudes the numerous qualities one may want in a man.

In Search of Ruth or Boaz

When we fill out an application, marital status stands out singularly as to how to address the applicant. Are you single, married, separated, widowed, or divorced? The inquiring minds of human resources, landlords, banks, corporate America, and our debtors want to know. But how important is marriage to the regular everyday folks? This is very important because churches and venues have events booked months, sometimes a year or two in advance, awaiting those special wedding days. While wedding nuptials are on a continuum, folks are also attending events of their parents, grandparents, or friends' anniversary celebrations, and vow renewals or have bragged about their parents' 25, 30, 40, or 50th anniversary jubilee. To listen to these lovely couples, reiterate respect, love, honor each other, warms our hearts. However, lately, the question has also become, why do individuals feel the need to be married? Even though folks still want to wed, the popularity of wedding bells is almost desperately trying to screech to a halt. Marriage gets a bad name; so, why marry at all?

It's the pushback on being told who and when to marry that is deterring some younger individuals from taking the plunge. While it is great to observe the techniques, lifestyle, and mannerisms of our parents who have experienced their family and developed a sense of themselves, the new generations seem to want to live their own lives, without being their parent's carbon copy. The parental baton is being passed down and sometimes after observing some of their parent's shenanigans, love, lies, and arguments, these young adults may have become confused. Sometimes, they may decide not to become duplicates, copycats, or copies of their parents. As a result, they may feel that many of those marriages were not good role models. They are also told to imitate them and fit into their mold, and the next generation should assimilate into culture and tradition. Hold up, not so fast! A marriage between two strangers can happen, but the option to choose whom to wed should not be an ultimatum.

Although intimacy, companionship, relationship, or a union may lead to wanting a permanent Ruth or Boaz in married life, it should not be coerced. While searching for such a partner or companion, certain individuals will always tell you what they think you ought to do, and how you should go about that search. They will project their feelings onto you. One of the reasons I am drawn to the Book of Ruth is because of her obedience to God. To be honest, I tried to find a suitable match for someone. In my biases, I was attempting to matchmake persons dear to me, because of selfish reasons. The simple fact was, I really did not want them to be alone. Once I die, they will have someone to share their innermost thoughts with. In my mind, it was that simple. I thought I would just make an introduction, then nature would take its course. There was no obligation or coercion involved.

We may not realize it at the time, but regret, pain, and the consequences of making the wrong choices eventually catch up to us. If someone is being forced to do something that goes against how they feel, it may be unnatural and unhealthy. This might make you very uncomfortable and unhappy. Unhealthy desires keep us away from God. So, put it this way, if it disrupts you inside, do not tolerate it, leave! Forcing the relationship might be detrimental to your well-being.

With divine intervention, matchmaking worked out for Ruth and Boaz, and it may work out for you, as well. It's a blessing for children to have the support from their parents. The support demonstrates a simple act of loving kindness. However, parents intrude because we are concerned about the welfare of our children.

* * * * * * * * * * * *

Chapter II

That's Just the Way It Is

In life, regret often plays a significant role in the categories of I should have, could have, would have, and if only I had... We all know that hindsight is 20/20. Hindsight allows us to see things with vivid color and clarity, but often only after it is too late or when the consequences become apparent. Everyone has an opinion about things that have nothing to do with them, taking on the roles of judge and jury in telling you, I told you so. This is almost laughable.

As young adults graduate from high school and prepare to enter adulthood, they will find themselves grappling with numerous questions about the direction their lives should take. These critical issues can range from simple to overwhelming, depending on individual thoughts:

- Do I need to stay locally because it is cheaper, or should I move to an out-of-state college?
- What college am I going to?
- Do I want to continue straight into college right out of high school?
- What do I want to become in 4 years?
- Should I date while I am in college?
- Am I going to live on campus?

- Will my high-school-sweetheart and I get married one day?
- Should I go to trade school?
- Will my parents mind if I go into the Armed Forces?
- Can I move out of Mom and Dad's house?
- How am I going to afford funds for college?
- Will I ever be independent?
- I want to travel!
- Will I be working this summer?
- Can I just hang out with my friends?

You are now a grown-up! This is known as adulting, whereby a lot of normal questions overwhelm the young mind and require immediate clarification but, somehow, become part of the clouds in the brain and subsequent unmentionables. When you can communicate your needs, reciprocate sharing, apologize for wrongs, take responsibility for your actions, and take care of your bills without imposing on others, you are an adult. Yes, no one mentions stuff like this, not even in a whisper. We just assume we have it all together but fail and spiral through life because those nagging thoughts and questions were presumed and never answered.

As young adults, some of us may turn to a school instructor, a pastor, a mentor, or our friends, however, it's the folks in our lives who have helped raise us, who may better help us figure it out. There may be fuzzy clouds, doubts, and no clarity at times, however, we muddle through.

Do we settle on what we are being told to accept without fully wanting to adapt? Many of us do. There is a saying, "mother knows best"! As the matriarch, mothers are the best diplomats. They must appease both husband and children to keep the peace. But, at some point, the cord must be cut by mom. I remember a friend telling me that she cannot be like her mother. The only response I could think of to tell her at the time was, you are not her, you are you!

This still resonates with me as the echoes of my past reverberate in my mind. Matters of the heart should be well thought out, especially when it will affect us personally. Choice is a major factor. We know what we do not want. However, since we may not be clear in knowing what we want, we may assume that every individual wants the best for their children. Parents mean well when they attempt to match their adult children with someone, whether it is the match suggestive or mandated? Ok, assuming that's true, I'll just pose this obvious question: We want the best for our children, don't we? Most unselfish parents and grandparents do, but we differ from the previous generation in that aspect. Our children will differ from us. Therefore, we should allow them to be who they are!

The micro-management of our children extends from birth, pre-school, kindergarten through high school. Some parents are not ready to detach. They assume they must keep interjecting and lead them in the direction they choose. Parents escort them right into college. In some cases, parents and grandparents put their time and effort into the younger generation, hoping that their children will reap the benefits from family values. So much goes into the foundation of our children. I am not a mathematician. However, there are a lot of parents', grandparents' halves, eights, fourths, and quarters involved in the ancestral make-up of a little human, plus the intention and rules we invoke on them, may be a bit much to take.

The expectations are great, and each part of these previous generations is linked or plugged into our children. Alright, perhaps not; let me stop laughing as I envision mom's nose, dad's personality, grandpa's hairy legs, grandma's wide hips, great-granddad's bowlegs as he walks, and great-grandma's fair skin passed down and try to add the parts together. Oh! Forget about if the math is not adding up, this child is born from the fibers of all that generational greatness, combined.

Albeit there's a point to be made here because I am today a mother who has grown into a grandmother who is passing on these inherent traits as well. Genetic make-up should be our defined contribution, which finds its way to our children, but today we want to either clone them into our own miniature likeness or marionette them into what we could not grow into.

In Search of Ruth or Boaz

What is the narrative? Parents really want to secure a better future for their children. Old-school, perhaps, but matchmakers state, "matchmaking worked for us. It will work for you, too!" Nevertheless, there is still that lingering feeling that they are pairing us up, not only for our security, but just to look good in society's eyes. Their image, family name and reputation are more important to them.

Most parents of earlier generations may have prayed for a large growing household who would help with chores, and other household matters and accept their children being in charge, as they enter their senior years, so that things would become less burdensome for them. In my case, my mom would say a Hail Mary to us, and would especially pray for her girls to have children of their own someday. She would say words like, "Girls take better care of their momma. Boys get wives, and well, if she is a good daughter-in-law, she may allow him to visit me at the nursing home".

As a child, listening to adult conversations, I thought it was hilarious. Of course, now that I am older, it's not so silly. In sincerity, times have changed indeed from needing dozens of children to help with chores or taking care of you in your old age. Social Security and investments in today's environment, have allotted our elders the affordability for accommodations for parents to independently live self-sufficiently in the over 55 communities, retirement communities, and then transition into assisted living facilities.

Now, young couples think about the expense of daycare, private schools, and the new question becomes: how many children can we afford after marriage? People are having fewer children; some individuals are having one or two offspring. Yet, parents are still clingy, so much so that parents are fearful of letting their children leave home because they fear they will never look for them in the rear-view mirror! It's not only the fear of disconnecting and having to commute across state lines or overseas, but the financial fear is also genuine, as well, because they feel that their children are their investments in the next generation.

In the old days, grandma and momma prayed back then, and I, along with my siblings, are a product of those answered prayers. With the best intentions, the cycle is to raise the children, and, after which, marry them off for them to have a family of their own, so that they will not remain alone. And, in step with continuity, in my case, my children are the next chapter in that reality! It begs the question: why do we push for folks to marry anyway? We have been saying to procreate, but child rearing has been happening with or without marriage. That is easily answerable. Folks marry and bond in a union for love, but there are tons of reasons why people marry. Although not in any order, they marry as follows:

- love
- sex
- family
- children
- immigration
- security
- companionship
- financial benefits
- ability to leave home
- health benefits
- grow old with someone
- hide their sexual orientation
- family obligations
- family matchmaking commitment

Of course, there are hundreds of other convenient reasons as to why folks marry. Family obligations and the promises made while they were, yet toddlers may come to roost.

Our parents cannot duplicate us and fit us into their mold, and we cannot be expected to robotically assimilate into culture and tradition. Folks will always tell you what they think you ought to be doing. Well, what about family obligations? Ok, what about it? We are obligated to provide for our family's immediate needs of food, clothing, shelter. There is no extended warranty to being hog-tied to payback obligations.

Family will project their fear onto you. It is up to us to know whether that is the baton we want to run the rest of life's course holding onto and passing to the next generation.

It is understandable that younger folks want to take their chance to experience the youthful nuances of their 20s and 30s. This is the stage in life to find out who you are, post-parents' house, and before settling down on your own. You know, the "me" era before any attachments. Men get a pat on the back during this time and call this the period of growing into themselves. So, how is this going to work out if there is already an imbalance? The ratio of men to women is disproportionately lopsided, as there are fewer men available to women for several reasons. Scarcity stems from incarceration, war, differences in mortality rate, etc. Statistics show there are shortages of men and, if I may mention, it is ladies who are being coaxed into marriage.

So, who is rushing these young ladies to settle down early? Where are they supposed to magically find these partners who are still sowing their wild oats? The young men have to be on that same page with the women. That is the only way this makes any sense. Men have more freedom to be. Women on the other hand, have always been more subject to stricter rules than men. The standard of holiness was elevated in a punishing mode for women. If it is not our hair, it is our clothing, make-up or jewelry, else risk being called a Jezebel. Women are influenced by not only their immediate families, but the input on their lives also come from family friends, spouses, even politicians.

Although the elders may have more of a profound say in these matters, it may be other people who may have nothing to do with their lives, which involve these marital societal pressures. The window for child-bearing biological clocks closes early, therefore, women are encouraged to marry earlier, else missing the opportunity of childbearing years. However, it still must be one's choice! We must analyze what works best for us. The decisions that we make in life do not have to have limits or place you in a cage. Poor decisions almost always lead to negative outcomes.

Oftentimes, parents and grandparents, although well intended, feel as if they are working against the clock, particularly if their children are over 35. In their wisdom, they know that the way of the world tells and shows us there will be daily challenges to overcome, and our children should not be alone to face them. John 16:33 These things I have spoken to you, that in Me you may have peace. In the world you will have tribulation; but be of good cheer, I have overcome the world".

After their children marry, grandparents look forward to having grandbabies. They may even salivate and dream about "a baby do-over" and getting to do the things they did not have a chance to do with their own children. They harp about our biological clock running out. You are becoming older, not younger. Those old eggs are fried by now. The awful triggers keep showing up, but this is not how to light a fire under our feet. It makes some of us more withdrawn.

This is where the planning and the plotting phase may take effect, and the plot thickens. Like scrambled eggs on a grill, it may get messy. These manipulative parents may involve the man of the cloth, and in-laws are also somewhere in the mix, to help seal the deal before their children are even dating.

This is a setup for failure, huh? No, there could not be any consequences for these underhanded schemes towards the matchmaking game. The parents' love for their children selfishly makes them take over the lives of their children. There is no ill-intent, however. The parent's narrative indirectly secures a future for their child with a stranger. They are from a good family, so my child will be ok. She is a good church girl and will take good care of you. They want us to marry a nice church girl or a nice church boy. Do they not know that the devil also attends church?

More importantly, did anyone ask… "Is he ready for marriage? Has the family prepared and developed their girl Ruth or boy Boaz for marriage? Have you trained your Ruth or Boaz for married life? Although it may sound sexist, have you wrecked your boy to expect a housekeeper in wife's clothing, or have you impaired your girl to be glamorous in appearance but not know how to boil an egg or wash her panties? Not sure if it matters, so long as the results are grandbabies. Oh, there's one other thing, did anybody ask, "what does this person want to do?"

You see, it's not about us, because as parents, we have had our turn! We must give in and compromise to what they want. To proceed any further would be potentially disastrous. Our fast-paced world does not allow us to stand by the Lord anymore because we take over the planning. Psalms 27:14 "Wait for the lord; be strong and take heart and wait for the Lord". I had observed an online wedding where a father gives his daughter away, but prior to handing her off to her future husband, begs the groom that should he no longer want her, please do not harm her, but return her back to him. Powerful tear-jerker, but heartbreaking.

I would love my children to be married. However, interjecting my desires may not be a good thing. And, if I am to be honest, I confess that I desire my children to have spouses who love the Lord and who will help be instrumental in guiding our family back towards God's grace. However, I have been led to believe and understand that it is the job of the Holy Spirit, not mine. The Holy Spirit is the only one who intercedes on our behalf. I needed to mind my business, as we often hinder ourselves by meddling, and by doing so, sometimes making matters worse. The desire for a life partner is also rooted in my blood as well as nursery rhymes.

If I remember correctly, I wanted to be a bride. I was the flower girl at my eldest sister's wedding, and all dressed up as the little bride. You know the adage of singing: “Going to the chapel and we’re going to get married!” I dreamt about it. I married my Barbie doll to Ken or a Ken-like GI Joe doll when I was a child, hoping one day it would be me! Naturally, I and millions of other little girls dreamt of being married, too. On that same note, I also know that not everyone will get married.

Oftentimes, folks may emphasize they never want to get married because they are self-sufficient. Are we indeed because no man is an island. Many of us go to God’s altar with our prayers; however, God can talk with us wherever we are and will see us through. The question is, are we listening? Currently, the Holy Spirit is telling me, “Hold up, wait a minute, now!” And guess what? I cannot be in my feelings and go ahead with my plans. Why? Because if I believe in a higher power, I must also know that I am not in charge, and I better listen to the man upstairs. I must learn to pray and tell God my needs and leave it to Him. Philippians 4:6-7: "Do not be anxious about anything, but in every situation, by prayer and petition, with thanksgiving, present your requests to God. And the peace of God, which transcends all understanding, will guard your hearts and your minds in Christ Jesus".

Having said that, I must also be patient and not rush God or want to help Him along. God does not need our help. The Holy Spirit is telling us that He is the one who is going to jump-start the fire in them for God. Proverbs 16:9 “A man’s heart plans his way, but the Lord directs his steps”. You cannot plan for God.

Jeremiah 29:11 "For I know the thoughts that I think toward you, says the Lord, thoughts of peace and not of evil, to give you a future and hope".

When our children become adults, should we continue to push both marriage and religion onto them? How did life work out for us that we want to project that road map onto them? Certain folks settle for less in a relationship because of past negative experiences and think this might be their last chance at love. We expediently rush into a relationship of our own accord because of loneliness, or we need to get away from a dire situation or are matched into it. The reason why is: we do not want to be alone. Whatever the reason, this will get us into deep doo-doo, as we wind up settling for far less.

Rushing and getting stuck in a bad relationship is foolish. God advises us to take our time. There is a song that says, "Momma Used to Say, Take Your Time Young M..." By taking our time, we can better understand the true essence of a person through their appearance, glances, comments, gestures, and over time be able to see through their disguise. Getting to know the person is imperative to the bonding process. However, we do not have to mold ourselves to fit into the relationship. But by wanting this so badly, we unknowingly make ourselves accessible to potential toxic behaviors. We do not want to hold still or pause. We want "no waiting" lines, or "express" and "expedite" signs. It's as if we feel we are going to miss out on something spectacular and are willing to sacrifice our innermost self to attain nothing. We often want instant results in order to be able to fit in with the crowd, while disregarding the advice of elders.

We neglect the Bible as well as the red flags, just to assume our friends have our best interests at heart, simply because we want to feel grown-up. We do not listen and want what we want. Following the advice of the crowd or our friends will lead to a dead-end sign. Acts 7:51-60 "You stiffnecked people, uncircumcised in heart and ears, you always resist the Holy Spirit. As your fathers did, so do you". Our parents are not always right, but it is still good to listen to advice, even if we keep it in our backpack for later use. We serve a higher power.

It is a good thing to want your children to serve the Lord, as you do. 3 John 1:4 "I have no greater joy than to hear that my children are walking in the truth. However, only the Holy Spirit can convict their spirit in the Lord". Ezekiel 36:26-27 "And I will give you a new heart, and a new spirit I will put within you. And I will remove the heart of stone from your flesh and give you a heart of flesh. And I will put my Spirit within you and cause you to walk in my statutes and be careful to obey my rules".

* * * * * * * * * * * * * * * * * * * *

Chapter III

Too Many Cooks Spoil…

No one has figured life out yet. Once you think you have it all figured out, there are going to be so many forks in the road that lead to split directions in life. Folks may not have a choice when the path is dictated to us; and in time, it seems that some of the ultimate choices may be made for us and not by us. Our paths may take its course at any time in our lives, including, but not limited to pregnancy, then at birth, while breastfeeding, while in daycare, during grade school, during a science course in high school, college, marriage, child-rearing, education, friendship, parenting, grandparenting, fostering, nurturing, not to mention self-realization because we are ever evolving. Ecclesiastes 3:1 "To everything there is a season, A time for every purpose under heaven: 2 A time to be born, and a time to die; A time to plant". Yes, we butt in and interfere in our children's lives.

To make matters worse, raising, meddling, busy-bodying, helicoptering, personality clashing, adding to that mix, places too many cooks in the making of an adult human, which spoils or stumps our children's growth. We have not learned to leave things alone and let them simmer by themselves to see the magnificence which life may derive. Nonetheless, no one ever stops to think that one day our children will become all grown up and will be detached from our loins and aprons. Since we still want the best for them, in our minds, we have that invisible puppet string or attached umbilical cord and are still attempting to manipulate and place an hourglass curfew around them. Unknowingly, this may strangle that relationship and make it estranged. Rather than pulling you closer, the relationship between parent and child may unravel and deteriorate. Since their future is at stake, allowing space and prioritizing your child's needs before yours is part of the greater solution to a happy and sustainable family and peace.

Some parents or relatives may get in the middle of a relationship because they disagree with a personal choice made due to someone's accent, religion, color, culture, or sex. For example, folks may say she is Dominican, and he's Haitian. They are not the right partner for you. She is bisexual, and he is heterosexual. You are working and they are unemployed. He is white, and they are black. She is Jewish, and they are Palestinian. You are a gay male, and she is a lesbian. She is Asian, and he is African American. You are Christian, and he is Muslim? Yes, in case it is not obvious, classism, racism, colorism, religion as well as sexism play a terrible part in deviating one's personal preference in love because it may not align with family standards. Does your family really know who you are?

Think about it, for a significant other not to be accepted by a parent because of their faith, class, race, ethnicity, or sexual orientation, is misguided and a huge blow to family dynamics because lines may have to be drawn as to which side they depart from. Labels limit, separate, devalue and isolate us. To have to make the choice one way or the other is impactful and unnecessary. Because of the heartbreak, there should be no picking sides. How does one get over that hump? Where does one start?

There is so much to unpack, however, you must love the person inside to be able to give love. Once you accept yourself and can love another, you are no longer hiding and are able to be free to love who you love. Listen, straight, gay, black, Hispanic, poor, white, Asian, tall, short, fat, thin, should not matter. God's love is unconditional and all-inclusive and our love for one another should be, as well. Romans 15:7 "Accept one another, then, just as Christ accepted you, in order to bring praise to God".

Firstly, it may be stated that this is just a phase, or this is not real. You may even get told: you will grow out of it. However, you should be able to enjoy every part of your relationship and enjoy living in the moment. Whether it lasts a day, a week, a month, a year, or a lifetime, ride the wave of love for as long as it lasts. Then they will ease into, well, how are you going to celebrate the holidays? Hurling the differences in culture and tradition at you, so that it will painfully sting. There are enough world conflicts and plenty of "I don't think you should…" This is where one would put a stop to the conversation because things are tough enough for those involved. Are you in love or should the question be, do you love them? Love is love! Ok, we know that love conquers all. However, if they are not into you, nothing will change that. It's important to find alignment in love, but also discussions amongst the individual involved parties, as outside sources and influences of life, will crush the relationship!

As parents, we do not understand that there is no right solution as to which way one should go in their relationship. The empathy part is to just listen to what your children are saying, without swaying their decisions. Accept their choice of partners, which means you accept them for who they are. The result of not meddling is that sometime in the future, it may lead to hearing stories from your children about relationships that brought them joy, or they may even get comfortable enough to discuss with you the wrong choices made or tell you about the girl or guy that got away. Listening and acceptance saves a lot of heartaches within the family. Or, if we shut them out, we may lose them completely due to our interference, disapproval, or non-constructive criticism of their choices.

Furthermore, we must reflect on choosing the wrong options that may truly affect the relationship with our adult children. In angst, they may depart from you. And, if they leave, there will be a quiet void in their heart that will miss you, should they choose the significant other. However, in some cases, no matter how hard everyone tries, that void will never be filled.

When matchmaking is not going according to plan, some parents may rant, what is wrong with them? I was married with five kids at their age, and they don't have one, yet! They need their player's card revoked. It's time to settle down. Is he ever going to get a job? What is, just kickin it? or why is she only focused on her career goals? Is she going to become an old maid?" One day, folks in these categories may have a change of mind and want to settle. Who knows? It is still a personal choice to be with the one you love. In relationships, there are categories and subcategories of married, single, widowed as well as divorce. For example, some folks may feel that they cannot be in a relationship with someone who already has children. Some deem them to have baggage and do not want to raise anybody else's children. The children would have a bonus dad or mom. However, they feel it is too complicated. But what if this person is the love of your life? There are those who love them enough to help them unpack.

A little story of the woman I called mom, a mother of six. When this man came into her life, I was not one-year old yet. She was hard on him because she did not want to play games. But the thing is, he was not playing. They became two peas in a pod. He loved her enough to stick around, marry her and helped bring up all her children to the United States. And, oh, they produced my baby brother.

Additionally, there are some folks who are just scatterbrained and just do not know what they want at that time, or even if they genuinely want to start a family. These folks are self-centered and less likely to be caring and giving to others. Although regrets may come into play later in life, they have a right to be self-centered, by choice.

Sometimes we fall prey to conniving, lying partners who may take advantage. Adulting graduates us into responsibility. There comes a time when we must take responsibility for poor choices in life. Certain folks may say, God bless the child that has his own; however, in a world of users, takers, lazy, carefree, sugar daddy, and sugar mamma seeking folks, child support seekers are so prevalent, there are too many naive folks who fall into their traps. Not to mention there are those who prey on the vulnerable, desperate, and lonely folks who are willing to settle for anything that says hello. If we are not careful, these takers and users can become sharers then take over everything you have. Knowing we deserve better is part of self-love. No dumpster diving allowed! Yes, our children unfortunately swim around a cesspool of selfish, fragile and frayed relationships.

Oftentimes, for lack of a better word, many of these children may have suffered from watching the examples we have set or are suffering from their own previously failed relationships. As a result, a bad relationship may cause our children to become reclusive, untrusting, or worse, never settle down with a partner due to fear that if you don't it might be your last chance at love. We want to help them, but do we jump in to help with the Superman cape to save the day? No! Well, why not? Then the question becomes: Why are you meddling? Why not let them find their own way? Spoiled brats? They're just dating and having meetups. Why do parents attempt to warn their children that the dating pool is a swamp? We want to prevent them from being eaten by Con Crocodile and Abuser Alligator. But you got bitten! Well, prevention is better than cure. That is why parents warn their children, to prevent them from going through the same nonsense. Will they listen? Perhaps. That is the cycle we want to break. It is not that simple especially when the children may become lost sheep because their parents were lost! That's prejudging. Ask yourself, am I a judgmental person? James 5:9 "Do not grumble against one another, brethren, lest you be condemned. Behold, the Judge is standing at the door". I just want my sons to be happy and settled while I am still young at heart. I guess I'm guilty of wanting them to be happy.

In some instances, marriage may not appear to be a priority for some who just want to live together and share expenses. I get that at times one may be undecided as to how to proceed in the relationship. Do we live together as dating partners? After all, what is the whole point of dating? The point of dating is to see if you like each other and how compatible you are! There is no judgment on someone who decides they want to play house. However, I have yet to understand when folks decide to live together rather than marry. They may state, it's a little contract or it's just a piece of paper or this paper doesn't prove my love for you.

What is even more odd, and what may drive certain folk's crazy is that after years of living together and they break up, they decide to marry the next person in the new relationship within months. Ask them, did that piece of paper suddenly change its meaning, or you just did not want to marry me?

Sometimes convincing us that marriage is only a piece of paper seems bogus until there is a sickness, illness, or death and you may not be permitted to attend because you are not a spouse or relative. If there are any doubts, there are other ways to ensure each other's personal finances. That is what prenups are about, in case stuff does not work out so you can't steal what does not belong to you! A partner may say, Let's live together before we get married so that we can get to know each other. This negates the fact that it does not happen while dating, courting, or the engagement period.

Dating is exploring possibilities. If it is not heading in the right direction, do not waste time because it is either working or it is not. Dating and engagement allow you to figure which person not to proceed in a relationship with or get married to. You may know deep in your guts that they do not want you. If after 5 years of dating, they do not want to commit to marriage, perhaps it's time to turn the page to a new chapter. Doormat or target practice is not a very becoming title. Giving ourselves away or allowing ourselves to be utilized, does nothing but prolong the inevitable collapse.

Ask yourself, what do I want and what am I getting out of this long-term nonmarital relationship? In other words, what is in it for me? I remembered the time that I had moved into my first ex-husband's apartment and left my momma's house. I was married but had no plans. My life's puzzle was being put together even before I understood the journey began. I was a kid myself and knew nothing about what to expect, or what was to come. I muddled blindly through this chapter of my life. When my son was born, I had to figure it out quickly. I had to become a supportive wife. Although unemployed, I became a stay-at-home spouse, managed our money, and became the best mom to our son, while my husband worked and attended school.

On the other hand, decades later, my second ex-husband moved in with me on the weekend after we were married. We decided it did not make sense to move into an apartment when I already had a house. At this point in life, I had a career, a home, grown children, and welcomed a contributing partner who would share life with me. Things may start off course, however, communicating and planning is important during trials and tribulation.

Yes, ok, right! Who am I to even join in on a conversation about this subject after two failed marriages? I did not have it all together. I did not know what was to come. No one does, and that is ok! Examples of my experience are not meant to scare anyone straight. We are all on different paths in life. Although this is not an advice column and I am sharing random thoughts, I must confess that I thought about finding matches for my children on a few occasions. As a person who is faithful in following God's guidance, it took a lot for me to consider discussing the topic of matchmaking on a personal level. I had to stop in my tracks and listen to the advice and allow the Holy Spirit to lead in this matter. Yes, reluctantly, I left the guys alone. Yes, it is up to them to decide for themselves. Ecclesiastes 3:10-11 "I have seen the God-given task with which the sons of men are to be occupied. 11 He has made everything beautiful in its time. Also, He has put eternity in their hearts, except that no one can find out the work that God does from beginning to end".

Although there are success stories of marriages and anniversary celebrations all around us, keep in mind that it takes a lot of nurturing to maintain them. Wow, that couple is celebrating their 40th wedding anniversary and we think, finally a marital bliss breakthrough, right? It is said that we notice their breakthrough but have no idea what they have been through to get to what folks consider successful because of the number of years spent married. Grandma had to get Grandpa out of that harlot's house not once, but on numerous occasions before he finally stopped cheating. She threatened her husband to put a stop to it. Is side-piece ultimatum a thing? Her husband may not be perfect, but he was perfect for her.

One thing that was set up between them was the conversation that she was not going to keep reminding him of his indiscretions, nor was she going to denigrate or emasculate him because of cheating, going forward in their marriage. He too, had to decide he was not going to cheat again. They both had to compromise, put the work in and not live as a married, single couple with mostly one person managing the household. Once they had that understanding, the marriage became stronger.

Even though he was the cheating spouse, she made a concerted effort to greet her husband like the king he is and never nagged. He made that same effort to treat her like the queen she is and never took her for granted. And now they've been married for over 59 years. If it is meant to be, even during hardship and disagreements, then it is meant to be! Many of us equate the length of time married to bliss and happiness, but it takes work! Love wins. Love is the only thing that matters.

We cannot see ourselves when we are going through it with a cheating partner because we are hurting. If our pain is not controlled, there will be hatred spewed, venom, even. The lenses become cloudy because we may see them as monsters who become the enemy. We sometimes state, once a cheater, always a cheater or if they are cheating with you, they will cheat on you. Perhaps those things may be true and to resolve the matter is a choice that may require mental health as well as pastoral counseling.

There are, however, lots of relationships which have recovered from the awful experience of unfaithfulness. And, although many do not turn out great, on the other hand, many have flourished. We think of a diamond when it comes in a box as a gift, how perfect it is; however, we never think about a diamond in the rough. For a diamond to shine, it goes through blasting, transporting, cutting then goes to get sized for whatever purpose. That is the same process that we go through in life and marriage. When a chapter ends, we must turn the page to continue the story into our journey. We quit without a fight. We want to shine without going through the process and that can never happen. Yes, sir, got to put the work in. That woman did not give up and held on tight, besides, who else was standing in line to help raise all those kids?

Marriages may survive loss, sickness, infidelity, meddling family members, unemployment, and long distance, to say the least. It is not successful from the snap of a finger; it takes two folks being committed and willing to work together during tough times. There cannot be two leaders in a relationship. If there is a commitment, you become a team. But there is no "I" in team. You must realize that you are not married to yourself. You are no longer one, in that marriage, discussions were had, and new promises were made, even though there were tough struggles to keep the marriage intact. Again, it takes work, who is up to the task?

Some of us have seen certain men in their 50s who have never been married and they are called, "the forever bachelor" or a "gigolo". In certain instances, those folks may eventually settle down when they are either old, broke, or ill, and they marry only because they need a nursemaid, not a partner. That is a fickle person, indeed, who changes his mind about dating and relationships, like he changes his Sunday outfits to be seen by many. Age does not always mean maturity. And nobody has time for fun and games. Although sometimes previous hurts prevent them from moving on but oftentimes one cannot make up their mind to grow in a relationship. Nevertheless, therapy and the willingness to find love again may turn that frivolous world into a calm oasis. James 1:7 "For let not that man suppose that he will receive anything from the Lord; 8 he is a doubleminded man, unstable in all his ways".

That is why finding Ruth or Boaz is like finding a needle in a haystack. A good life partner is hard to come by period! Everyone is searching for someone to enhance their lives. However, even with the help of million-dollar dating companies and apps, matchmaking parents and friends, accidental haphazard meetings, grandma setting you up with a nice person from church, college campus dorms, bonfire gatherings, and bar hopping, for numerous reasons, there is a huge disconnect as to why it's hard to find that ideal partner.

I know someone who met, fell in love with, and married their junior high school sweetheart. They have been married for over 45 years. I have also seen high school sweethearts who promise to remain together forever, go haywire. They left home to attend different schools in the hopes that they would grow and receive respective degrees and accolades, after graduation, never to see each other again. I have also seen those who made promises to accomplish their goals, but when they did not mesh upon returning, were willing to let go and go their respective ways. There were no sparks and certainly no obligation to remain miserable in the relationship. However, once everyone has moved on, it may not be prudent to compare a future relationship with that past, especially since the relationship did not work out.

Is it safe to say that being single sometimes places the players, nerds, and conceited, antisocial folks in one cluster? There may be too much machismo, too little oomph and introversion, or some folks wanting to remain alone and in their comfort zone.

The latest excuse being utilized is well, I'm not sure if I'm "financially ready" at 40? One is either ready for a relationship, or they are not. One may say her biological clock is running out! However, are we rushing to check these boxes because of societal pressures? We forget to live in the moment of making great memories that we can savor and keep building on. We cave into the pressures and place goals of what we are supposed to attain at a certain age, check! Who says we must accomplish this at 35? There are no excuses necessary when one does not want to enter a relationship. Why? Because that category is bogus. If one amasses wealth in the millions, one may still say that they are not ready, and guess what? There will always be a reason as to why. No one wants to hear "because I don't want to". So, what? Who cares? Still remain yourself because it's your life! On the other hand, there are many single younger folks, who may at times, whine and complain about, "woe is me. Out of all my friends, I can't be the only one by myself. I can't find anybody, I'm tired of being by myself". I also know that not everyone wants a partner. Some people choose to be single on purpose. Other people, after being alone, opt in for a pet. As a matter of fact, I had a friend tell me, "My dog is my loyal baby". He went on to say, "My ex and I broke up, and I got to keep the dog. I am in no mad rush to start a new relationship". I thought about that, and this man did not settle for a piece of his girlfriend, nor did he say, well, some of her is better than none of her. He happily took the dog and went about his business. I don't think that there is anything wrong with this at all. After a tumultuous breakup, there are those who feel as if they got that memo and understood that they would rather remain by themselves, than be with someone ratchet. In other words, I can do badly all by myself. It's intentional and I respect that. Not everyone is meant for a match or meant to have a partner in life. 1 Corinthians 7:8 "Now to the unmarried and the widows I say: It is good for them to stay unmarried, as I do. But if they cannot control themselves, they should marry, for it is better to marry than to burn with passion".

It is up to us to know if we are up to the task of letting our children make their own decisions. What is the worst thing that may happen if one partnered up or never partnered up with your chosen match? Well, the truth of the matter is that they might become lifelong friends, or they may acquire a pen pal, or they may agree to marry your old neighbor's offspring back home. On the other hand, indirect matchmaking may not work either as they might not take the bait, but at least you may feel better because you would have tried to help someone you love. Nevertheless, stop making matchmaking solely about you. Notice the key words reflect your personal feelings and not your child's. That is not good!

Furthermore, who said it is not ok to remain single? Adam was lonely, so God took a part of him to form Eve. We have the option to remain alone, and others want to be a part of a whole. Society shames folks for wanting this. There is nothing wrong with being alone. One is complete if alone. There is no imperfection in oneness because you are whole. The old-maid syndrome should be thrown out the window.

In addition, there are also the newly divorced or widowed group, and there are those who just do not want to get married. There are those with personality traits that may pinpoint why they are single. Lest we forget, not everyone is a wordsmith, charismatic, charming or a schmoozer. We can further say that some folks are shy or can be introverts. Some folks prefer to be alone and just play video games. They don't want to go to the gym to meet people, because the truth of the matter is they are uncomfortable. They may not have the money for a proper date. They are not smooth and do not go to the club because they can't dance. And perhaps the same goes for church socials. They are tired of looking for excuses to validate why they are or want to remain single. There will be an endless number of excuses given as to why folks want to be single. Look, it's great if that is what one likes. These are not the typical user gigolo singles. We do not have to make any excuses if we decide to remain single, as long as we do not mess with other folk's lives. Be that great single person. Be you!

At any rate, I have to say one should not be in a relationship, just to avoid being lonely. This is not cool, and it is also compromising the next person. Your heart should sincerely be in it. However, one should always keep in mind that lollygagging for years and simply wasting part of our limited 65 to 75 winters of the average lifespan can never be replenished again. Once those years are lost on the youth, it's wasted time gone forever. Perhaps one day there will await a suitable match. You never know because our heart has perfect vision, but time works against us, as the hourglass is not infinite. Let's not waste it.

These young adults just need a nudge or a jumpstart. Finding a partner for your children is archaic and old school, isn't it? Yet various ethnic groups are still in the matchmaking game. What's wrong with them? I am not one to say, but one of my answers would be, "Absolutely nothing!" Some may say that is a desperate move! But you must admit, wanting your child settled and secure in life with a partner is not a bad thing. Many parents don't seem to think there is anything wrong with the supposition. However, we should also understand that we should not put on our super capes and intercede on their behalf or at least frown upon the thought of doing so each time it enters our minds. We should also think that superimposing our personal thoughts and beliefs onto our grown children is not fair to them. We had our chance to do what we wanted to do with our lives, and eventually, I did.

Most of us want the best for our children. Nevertheless, after we observe their indecisiveness, we may want to ask them, "What do you want for yourself or where do you see yourself in 5 years?" One of the most profound questions should be, "Is this what you want?" and if so, "are you ready to commit?" Then tell them, "I support whatever you want". Believe it or not, your statement will go a long way in your relationship with each other.

Many of us pass the baton of contribution from the ancestors to our children and theirs. With all the buffoonery and misinformation out there, I trust my own judgment. Normally we would not meddle between 18 to their mid-20s because our children are attempting to find themselves. They should be given an opportunity to experience life and see how they handle dating, marriage, and ultimately family. Our children may be in marriage number one or two and have either not produced children or do not want any. Although this is a whole other conversation, it is their business. Nevertheless, at midlife, if this has not happened, it is not necessary to recreate the narrative by intervening, even if there may be a possibility of them missing the rainbow of having children entirely. There is no straight answer or point of view on this subject matter. The only option is to simply plant a seed, give it sun, water it and tomorrow it will flourish!

Deep down our parents do not want us to face life alone. In this manner, they acquire an urgency to light a fire under their children's feet to run and find a life partner. They start thinking, eating, and dreaming of marriage and babies running rampant before they die. For these parents, now it's time to settle down. However, one day, folks in these categories may see clearer, and reconsider. Who knows? What's the point? Well, settling for whatever, just so you will not be alone; being in a loveless marriage; or facing financial burdens, may not have been a well-calculated option. It would hurt a parent more to see their children suffering while married. Nevertheless, no one can tell someone to remain or leave an unhealthy relationship. This, too, is a personal choice, as what works for this person may not be appropriate for others.

I'm going to give a tiny example of a personal choice: I had a choice of staying in an unhealthy and toxic marriage when I found out my husband of seven years was not only unfaithful but was cheating with numerous women. Although he was a good provider, I had to decide the pros and cons that would be beneficial for me. Was my health being compromised? Did I want to stay in this mess? Folks never put soul ties into perspective. When there is cheating in a marriage you are technically in bed with different people. That oneness or connection in lovemaking with your spouse is gone because the soul is wandering. The soul is lost. Furthermore, the sad part is that the sidepiece did not mind existing as his secret. Everyone knew of his secret and laughed behind my back. I had to think of what was best for me and subtract and remove all the negative energy. One of the questions I had to ask myself was, "who did I marry?" Once I knew of the affair, there was such a great metamorphosis when I looked at him. I saw him as a monster who did not care for my well-being. I could not remain accessible to his toxic behavior, and I thought, "was I financially stable enough to be on my own? Was I willing to lose myself to please him"?

Yeah, the struggle would be real, but was I worth it? Unlike thousands of women who may be in the same situation, I did not have young children. Therefore, I chose for him to leave. Am I happy to be on my own? No! Do I feel alone? No! Am I lonely? At times. Did my ex-husband change? No! Did I make the right decision? Hell, yes! I am paraphrasing but I once heard Ms. Maya Angelou say in an interview, "when someone shows you who they are, you had better believe it". And with regards to deception, nothing would have changed with this little poor man. Certain folks have no originality, as they continue to use the same playbook to play games. So, I had to make that choice back then and it was the right one for me. I had to start on a new journey of healing.

Thousands upon thousands of people go through soul tie issues and the thing is many of us have had our heart broken through infidelity, however, many remain with heart-filled hate and bitterness from that experience. When your heart is sour or bitter, the ripple effect is ginormous. The darkness from this envelops you enough to not only eat you up from the inside, but it spreads onto others in the form of hate. Therefore, don't let your heart stay bitter because you want to grow to become a better person. That is the only way to allow yourself to heal. These cheaters have moved onto their next escapades. Harboring ill will is not healthy. We must allow a healing spirit to enter our heart before starting a new relationship and moving on. Psalms 34:18-19 "The Lord is near to those who have a broken heart, and saves such as have a contrite spirit. 19 Many are the afflictions of the righteous, but the Lord delivers him out of them all".

The plan and foundation of marriage matchmaking may have been set by others since birth. Planning or controlling someone else's life may not be a wise move. Anyone who feels doubt or unease about an arrangement should at least have a conversation with the host about the elephant in the room. Your choice may or may not align with theirs, therefore, it is prudent to set all the facts in place for discussion. Like it or not, either way, the ultimate choice should be yours!

Anything that causes stress during the dating stage, put it down. When a relationship drains your spirit, move on. Leave the past behind because that spirit cannot enter your new household. Think about this as discarding an old mattress with bed bugs. You do not want your new house to be infested. If not dealt with, these issues will cause restlessness and anxiety. Again, letting go of past relationships because it no longer serves a purpose for you, will not only allow you to release old junk, but it will also make room for you to embrace and nurture the new relationship. When we lose touch and paths change or we choose to leave someone behind, it is for a reason. In some cases, we may regret what we did not get to do and the chances we didn't take. The curiosity of what ifs lingers. We may miss what we have chosen to leave behind. However, when we have dealt with the past and learn to let these memories go, perhaps we may not regret the choices we made.

* * * * * * * * * * * * * * *

Chapter IV

I Felt Him

For as long as I can remember, I have always felt a strong connection to God. From an early age, I felt a tug and pull in my heart, urging me to draw closer to Him. It is as if the Holy Spirit was gently tapping on my shoulders, persistently calling out to me. Looking back, I realize that I yearned to remain close to God, like a second skin. Although I could not fully comprehend it at the time, I found solace in the warm embrace of His love and grace. Yes, even at that early age, I knew. My belief in God does not exclude me from the inconsistencies of this earthly life. I refuse to listen to the naysayers who forget that life is going to do what it does with everyone on earth. However, when the love of God is in our heart and we go to Him in prayer, He will be with us during the trials of life. I do not question, "why me?" God loves me unconditionally and that is what keeps me whole and sane in my journey.

I distinctly remember the moment I knew I wholeheartedly loved the Lord. I was about 8 years old, attending a Catholic Church in Brooklyn, New York. Having spent my early elementary years in an all-girls Catholic school in Haiti, this was a new experience for me. It was during one of those vibrant church services that I encountered an enthusiastic Haitian priest, leading the congregation in songs and dance to praise the Lord.

This priest's energy was contagious, and I found myself joyfully clapping and dancing along to the lively contemporary gospel tunes. I knew right then and there that I wanted to be a part of this joyful celebration of faith. While my mom didn't share the same enthusiasm for attending church or walking the long blocks from Sterling Place to Classon, she made sure that we attended every Sunday. Her commitment ensured that I had the opportunity to experience these uplifting moments of worship and connection to God. When we moved to Queens in my teen years, I found a broader religion in terms of the norm of singing, swaying, and dancing in church. I got another dose of continuity to keep my veins hydrated and connected to God in a wider community setting. My new friends, who had attended a Methodist church, invited me to come along. At this point, everyone in my house wanted to sleep and rest on a Sunday morning. I was the only one in the family who was interested in waking up early enough to catch a ride to attend church service. A few years later, after moving back to Brooklyn, I simply stopped attending church, again. There was a large gap where I did not attend church at all for years.

Years later, even after I got married in a Catholic church, I did not continue to attend church service. However, it was around the time when my eldest son was around five years old when I reconnected with the church. Proverbs 22:6 "Start children off on the way they should go, and even when they are old, they will not turn from it". At 25 years old, there was a constant tugging, and truth be told, not only was I empty, but that burning fire in my heart for God was aflame.

I have always looked for God even at my darkest moment when the evil one whispered, "Where is your God now," I felt enveloped in his arms, even when I was being led astray. Don't get me wrong, the storm clouds, rains, and even the tsunamis took me under to where I didn't want to run in the directions to where I believed God would be. Nevertheless, even when I was lost, the greenery around me, just like sunshine, would blossom, after the flood of my problems receded. God always had that special hold on me. My life had highs and lows of dark tunnels and high-flying kites in the sunshine. I was never allowed to stay comfortable in a mess.

If you are alive, something good or bad may pop up. Life does not mean that you won't go through it, it just means you have enough faith to know that He will carry you and be right by your side while life happens. Are you a believer? If so, you know that life is ever changing.

I got married at 19 to the man whom I was dating because we were going to have a baby. Oh, never mind how that happened. At the time I was in love, but I wouldn't dare tell my mom, "No" when she said, I was going to have to marry this man. She mumbled, in what was gibberish to me at the time, "You are my last baby girl and the first one to get pregnant". The other three girls were married and out of the house at the time. I really believe that was why I didn't hear the end of the endless cursing from my mama and in my Haitian culture at the time, the gentleman caller who was drinking my mom's calf's milk had to buy the entire cow.

She has seen the worst in life and wanted better for me. Heifer, goat, young woman, my momma was the whole herd, as she was not going to take no for an answer when she stated there was going to be a June wedding. Seriously, though, I was her last baby girl, and she wanted to honor me, in her mind, as Mrs. Somebody! I may not have agreed, but I respect her for that. My mama booked and scheduled the church, wedding gown fitting, guest list, reception, and after the ceremony, I had to say goodbye to my mama because I was a married woman now. I was a young bride. Ironically, we were married the year Cyndi Lauper was singing “Girls Just Want to Have Fun”.

Years went by and in between those nuptial dots, we had two boys. He was a waiter who became an accountant, and I was a stay-at-home mom. Trust and believe the struggle was real in patching the funds and making pennies stretch. I eventually went back to school to contribute to household expenses. Unfortunately, our goals and dreams were deferred not only in terms of career but also in husbandry obligations and priorities. He left the country and started a whole new life in the Caribbean. I attempted to be both mother and father in raising two boys in the rough streets of Brooklyn. Thus, we parted ways and divorced decades later because he would not sign the divorce papers. In hindsight, time sped us through life's roller coaster, and we lost sight of the marriage.

I'm not going to fill in all the blanks, however, after meeting my first husband in college at 18, I may not have had a draft and potential plan for us, and as a young woman, I'm not sure if I wanted to marry so young. I know everyone wants to find their person, however, due to my unplanned pregnancy, I was nudged by my mom to have a formal wedding. Technically, it was not an arranged marriage because I was already dating this man. I was in love at the time, and my mom formulated a match with the person I was already associated with and had bonded with. This anecdote differs in that this was a dude I was with, had lunch in the park, studied together, had walks on the beach with, smelled, tasted, and loved. We were forced to speed up the marriage due to a child coming in the next few months. I was not blind sighted with an unknown fiancée and chaperoned the night before and married the next day. We were going to have a child and thus believed there was nothing we could not get through together.

Did I choose and agree to the best match for myself? I don't know. What I know for certain is there is no right person or best match I can forge, but Father God who is the ultimate planner, knows best. Besides, my children had to come through our two vessels. Raising my children from such a young age has had such a tremendous impact on my life, and I would not have changed a thing because of them.

In Search of Ruth or Boaz

The trajectory of my life changed when I became pregnant. My Haitian mother stepped in and redirected my path to becoming a teen bride at 19. Thus, I must say even though matches are summoned, matchmaking's ultimate decision is for the two involved parties to agree upon. I have no regrets. There are certain cultures that have arranged marriages, there are children who are matched and promised to another family from birth without any knowledge of the young people involved. Although some of those marriages may fail, the majority of those arranged marriages work.

Love. We need that human interaction. Most of us are looking for a good partner, whether we want to admit it or not! I understand what may work for some does not work for others. Besides, who am I as a twice-divorced woman to be throwing my response or even my feelings into the hats of anyone's choices? Being twice divorced may even disqualify me from commenting on this subject, I don't know. I can suggest what not to do! That's a lie because everyone's experience is unique to them, and no one should compare apples to oranges. I have had to start over, not once, but twice. I know that even though my life's journey was directed by the Lord, my choices may have been poor as well, and there are consequences. Throughout all of it, God remained steady by my side. Hebrews 13:5 "...For he Himself has said, 'I will never leave you nor forsake you". So many good and bad things happened in my life, and however bad, it could not be any other way. Nevertheless, within this journey called life and the choices I made, I realize that I was not starting over, I was starting with life experience!

Life's struggle is real, and some of us may want a partner to help shoulder the responsibilities of marriage and running a household. Ecclesiastes 4-9:10 - 9 "Two are better than one, because they have a good return for their labor: 10 If either of them falls, one can help the other up. But pity anyone who falls and has no one to help them up". I wanted to please God, but the choices that I made in getting married were also for society. I believe that my first marriage was forced upon me by my mother because she was embarrassed that I was unmarried and pregnant at a young age. I have to also be accountable, as well, because I was not in a position to raise a child alone.

The second marriage, even though I was mature and should not have allowed myself to be coerced, was to please the church and I did not want to sin in God's eye. It did not make any sense that I procrastinated and said no so many times. It should have been a sign to end the relationship and not remain tied. There were red flags in our age difference, our varied work schedules, and so many other factors. I allowed myself to get comfortable and succumb not only to his pressures, but also denied my doubts. People pleasing, especially when these folks should be minding their own business, always leads to a disastrous journey because folks get married for the wrong reason. But as one of the parties involved in both marriages, I convinced myself otherwise and did not stand my ground. Therefore, I, too, have to say that I was and am part of the problem which failed my marriages. As Penny Reid stated, "You are not required to set yourself on fire to keep other people warm". That analogy of people-pleasing at the expense of my well-being has stuck with me.

Going forward, I know that I matter more than what others may think or project on me! Many of us believe that marriage is a great thing. And it is! 1 Corinthians 7:1-5 "It is good for a man not to touch a woman. 2 Nevertheless, because of sexual immorality, let each man have his own wife, and let each woman have her own husband. 3 Let the husband render to his wife the affection due her, and likewise also the wife to her husband. 4 The wife does not have authority over her own body, but the husband does. And likewise, the husband does not have authority over his own body, but the wife does. 5 Do not deprive one another except with consent for a time, that you may give yourselves to fasting and prayer". In this union of marriage, there should be a natural flow of love. One should be able to lean on the other partner. When things go awry in a relationship, a marriage is worth fighting for. It's simple, I'm sorry, baby. A sincere apology, discussing what happened with no insult, be clear and direct by candidly speaking your mind, resolving it, and then let's make up. Pride has no place here. Proverbs 16: 18-19 "Pride goes before destruction, and a haughty spirit before a fall. 19 Better to be a humble spirit with the lowly, than to divide the spoil with the proud". Giving it your all means giving your best towards reparation.

In Search of Ruth or Boaz

After attempting to salvage a marriage, or when one has tried hard enough to keep it afloat, we acquire scars. Sadly, these scars were from loved ones. What happens when scars build up, we get scar tissues. As these scar tissues multiply, we get a block. This may cause further damage, even though scars are a part of healing. In other words, do not let it build to a point where the caring stops and the relationship is not salvageable. Before this happens, let's talk about it to start the healing process…

Figure it out!

* * * * * * * * * * * * * * * * *

Chapter V

Who is Boaz to Me?

Let's get one thing straight, Boaz was not a God. I understand that no man is perfect, however, he was an ideal man characterized in the Bible. He was masculinity wrapped up in one. Boaz was single, mature, respectful, unafraid of hard work, a boss, caring, and actively looking for Ruth, his spouse! Respect is very important in any relationship, and Boaz championed respect.

What makes a man, a man and a father? When a man reaches a stage of completeness, surpassing puberty and fully embracing adulthood; it's not just the ability to father a child, as any functioning sperm bearer from a tween can accomplish this task, but when he can embrace the responsibility that comes along with that life, that is when he is ready to be a man. The extension to that is he becomes a provider, a father, a contributor, a husband, a lover, a defender, and a family man. He is an adult human being who exudes strength, love, and the warmth in his embrace covers his household. When we are asked, 'Who is that man?' A simple response, for some, may be 'That is my dad, husband, brother, son, grandfather, cousin, uncle, mentor, etc. Boaz was the all-around man, which many who are looking for the ideal husband, want in their life.

In Search of Ruth or Boaz

In Biblical terms, Boaz was a serious and mature man. He was older, yet vibrant and hardworking. He accepted his inheritance and assignment as the family redeemer to make sure everything not only got done right but was also legal in the sight of the law. His attributes were that he was a manager, provider, protector, planner, selfless, caring, honest, thoughtful, trustworthy as well as a responsible leader. He thought of others first. He also shouldered the responsibilities of his clan without complaining.

Ask yourself, is my ego so big that all I think of is myself. We overestimate how hard this is to do, even when he didn't want to, but mustered the courage to keep helping everyone. Boaz was not a boastful man and kept his pride and ego at bay. Boaz did not have anyone to go home to listen to his thoughts and feelings. He was alone and wanted a wife.

Boaz has been looking for the right woman for years and has not found her amongst the lot, even though he is a man of resourcefulness. He owns land, and not only that, but he also makes it his business to know who is working in his fields and how the handlers are properly running his crops and properties.

First, he noticed and inquired about who this new young woman was who was harvesting on his property because he knew that he hadn't hired her. Once he received the information on her, he eased up, and made her more comfortable to work there. Not only that, but he also covered, protected, and made sure no one touched or did her harm. He noticed that Ruth had good ethics, morals, and cared about her mother-in-law, who was related to him through her deceased husband. Boaz is a man who takes pride in being a provider. He was dedicated to serving others selflessly and always looked out for the well-being of both his family and his community. He was genuinely compassionate and had the heart of a lion. This gentleman felt personal responsibility towards his clan. This is also a praying man over his household, and that makes him even more attractive in character.

Although he was lonely, he never used his status to get women. He was not a player. It is presumed that Boaz may have had a family and lost them, similarly to how Naomi had lost hers. We assume that men do not suffer loss, or suffer loss differently from women, but there was a lot of pain inside Boaz. Hurt is hurt! Presumably, missing his family, he delved into work to keep himself preoccupied.

Not all men go to the immediate bed warmer to help them in their mourning state. Although there are songs and actions by some ladies that scream, girls are players too. The bad-boy image may be prevalent as some want to be seen with one, even though a lady knows it's temporary or the relationship might last a few months, at best, the money man and bad-boy image still attracts certain women.

Boaz, however, was a great man of morals and character. His marital status at that point in time in the Old Testament was not discussed, however, bible discussion just makes assumptions that he was single at this time since there was no mention of it. However, one may wonder, if Boaz was such a law-abiding redeemer, why did he not marry Naomi, who was a closer relative than Ruth?

It may also be assumed that Naomi was older and an unlikely choice to give birth to a child, at such an advanced age. Ruth, however, would still represent the family clan, thereby redeeming his kin. Boaz did not have to be reinstructed on how to be a good husband. If I am not mistaken, he must be at least in his sixties, if not older as he tells Ruth, I respect that you are not frivolous and are not chasing after younger men. Ruth 3:10 "Blessed are you of the LORD, my daughter!" Boaz exclaimed. "For you have shown more kindness at the end than at the beginning, in that you did not go after young men, whether poor or rich". He admired Ruth and seemed to care for her even more because the young men would not be his rival. Boaz is a respectable, disciplined, and law-abiding man who wants to be her caretaker, provider, and her helpmate. However, he had to abide by the law, as there was someone in her stepfather's line as head of the clan, who had more rights to marry her first.

This was an educated and wise man who was in a high position in his clan. Yes, Boaz was an older man, and had been taking care of everyone else's needs, but his own. He was preoccupied with handling the business, just to cover the deadness he felt on the inside. No one before Ruth showed him care, and such boldness in having any interest. He may have felt folks liked him for the things he could provide.

Ruth, however, stood out and he felt her presence. She was the one and he knew it immediately. Ruth startled him and awakened him! She made him feel that he was not dead inside. He was elated because Ruth showed that she was interested in him. As a man, he must have felt alive again and knew someone wanted and needed him. From the perspective of a man, it sparked Boaz's interest and elevated his ego.

When a man is interested in a woman, there are more than sparks that fly and a tingle. He cares about her wellbeing. Is she ok? Did she eat? Is it observable that this man exhibits his feelings, wants, and strives to provide, share, and care? Note these questions in your mind with regards to, "Does he have the capability to bring greatness to the table? Is he lazy and expects to be the homebody while you are at work or in school? Are there expectations from you about what you can provide? Are family togetherness and values important?"

Boaz saw a spirit of selflessness in Ruth towards her mother-in-law that he admired. When he first saw her, he probably did a double take and wondered, who is she?

Imagine a date with this man in 2023! Boaz's face lights up when she enters the room. In anticipation, he cannot wait to hold her hands. He cannot wait to rest his head on her shoulder to smell her perfume. They talk about everything under the sun as they get to know each other, setting the tone on likes, dislikes, how they feel and what they would expect in a relationship. After dropping her home, I'm sure he can't wait to hear her voice again, because he does not want to send her an impersonal text. He already misses Ruth and wishes he could give her a comforting hug. In his mind, he is already planning their next dinner date or picnic, beach outing, going to church, walks in the park, and getting to know her likes, dislikes, and favorite colors, wondering what her family values are.

Boaz is thinking like a calculator as his pheromones not only heighten for this partner, but she is all he is thinking about because she has attracted his undivided attention. You may be wondering; how does she do that? She has shown she cares for the welfare of his kin, she is hardworking, she is faithful, and has a great reputation. Not to mention that he was enamored with her. Ruth just simply enters a room, and Boaz melts. Ruth was not overlooked, because he sees her in her entirety. Boaz observes the color of her eyes and supple skin, her long flowing dark hair under the headscarf, how she walks on air. Yes, Ruth made his imagination run wild. He not only saw her presence, but Boaz also really grew to love her! As a man, he thought, "I want to marry this woman". He is thinking how can I show up for her and what are her immediate needs? He made sure she and her mother-in-law had enough to eat, without it seeming like a handout. Boaz loved and was in awe of Ruth immediately. Love is an emotion that cannot be controlled. It is more than physical, although the eyes are not blind, but are pleased.

Boaz knew that his search for his perfect match was over. His pursuit of her was a need towards permanence and he wasn't chasing a temporary girlfriend to dispose of for the next chase. He had finally found Ruth. Boaz is like a floating cloud with a steady radar. He knew immediately that this person was going to be a partner. He knew that he was next in line in the clan, to claim Ruth. For Boaz and by today's standards, it does not take years of engagement and living together. He knew he would commit to her. When you know, you know! "This is the one," he confirmed to himself. This is not a trial and error or a trial fitting room for potential partners. It is more than a feeling when you look into their eyes. There will be no doubt that this one will be my forever boo! Once your gaze is locked in, there is no preset blueprint because the eyes will not lie.

With all the narcissists, users, and fake it 'til-you-make-it folks out there, there are not a lot of fish in the sea who are truly qualified to be a total package Ruth or Boaz. Finding someone who will be mentally, emotionally, financially, and physically there for you is rare. There are no pre-programmed robot partners set to do this. We must take the time to talk, smell, feel, and like a person to allow them to feel our soul. If this person is enamored with you and can take the time to put their plans, business trip, or even their important cell phone aside to prove that they care, then give them a chance.

Boaz was consistent. He did not wish he could get Ruth, nor did he remain idle, hoping this would come to fruition out of thin air. Boaz sprang into action. He dropped everything that day, to claim Ruth as his. He did not waste the time because life is short. Therefore, Boaz felt the competition was on. Boaz exemplified masculinity and power. He probably thought to himself, I'm going to prove my love to her, claim and marry this woman. And, not wasting any time, Boaz ran to the community gathering that same afternoon to clarify familial belonging, because he knew immediately that he wanted to have Ruth as a wife. There was no delay, or stating, I will get to it later. He acted swiftly because he knew he had hit the jackpot! He willingly risked going public. There was no shame in his game, and he was going to make it plain to the entire community to find out what the other man's intentions were before he could move on with his. This was both a selfish and selfless act because he was going to do the right thing under the law. Boaz knew that when someone was important enough, he had to find a way. He found a way because Ruth mattered to him. He was willing to take that risk, even if he was going to get his heart broken, should that redeemer have chosen to keep Ruth as his own.

So, the clarification and declaration were made in front of elders and the question he basically asked, "Do you have any intent or interest in marrying this woman? If not, then clap those shoes and Ruth will be mine". So, Boaz elevated the name of his clan and kept it honorable and respectable. Boaz was nervous and did not know what the outcome would be. However, he took charge and kept his promise once he became the redeemer, and he could marry Ruth. This would grant him the ability to place her under the umbrella of being protector, provider, and procreator with the woman who wanted him, as well.

Let us put it out there, just saying, not every man is ready to be a man. The questions should be asked: Is this person who you consider as a partner still exhibiting selfishness, conceitedness, laziness, frugality, flirtation, self-serving, anger, or narcissistic qualities? Does he want to play house? Then he is not ready to become a husband! When a man is ready, he will put forth all that energy and excitement into the woman he loves. She is not an afterthought.

Boaz is that man we should be looking for. So, yes, is he into you? On the other hand, if he is not into you, nothing will change that because he can keep you low and mistreat you or just use you. But if he loves you with all his being, he will put your needs first. He will put as much effort into you as he would into something that he admires and cares for. His actions will align with what he says. He will keep you on such a high that you will never want to come down from.

Boaz loved this woman aloud. His love for her was unconditional and not dependent on anything. He is honorable, faithful, and a man who will not only love his wife, but make sure her well-being is taken care of. Boaz was indeed ready to commit to one woman, Ruth. He made it known that she was his and took that chance and prayed that the original redeemer would not take the woman he loved. He fought for and got his Ruth. She would be forever his! They became two peas in a pod!

* * * * * * * * * * * * * * *

Chapter VI

A Woman Named Ruth

Ruth was a widow. In other words, she had been married, however, her husband had died, and she had not produced a child yet during that marriage. Ruth had a servant's heart and was family oriented, loyal, diligent, intelligent, and a forward thinker. Ruth had never portrayed herself as needy or a damsel in distress. She was optimistic and full of life and had a never-giving-up spirit of enthusiasm. She was a virtuous woman who adopted the faith she married into and then became a widow at a very young age. Ruth stuck around and was reliable, even after her husband died. She felt committed to her mother-in-law. Under no circumstances did she abandon her mother-in-law, Naomi! For as long as I can remember, this has been one of the best love stories in the Bible for me because of her trust and obedience to God.

Although I am not making Ruth out to be a saint, I must point out that when she looked to go back to where she had come from, she wondered what she had to go back to. The men were not exactly tripping over themselves in finding her to bring her back. Where were all these men exactly? She must have thought, at least I would have a better chance returning with my mother-in-law, who had been good to me while I was married to her son. She wondered in her mind, was there a crowd from my village waiting to take me in? Ruth attempted to bring her sister-in-law with her.

Her sister-in-law probably thought the total opposite and decided, without much prodding, that she was going to take her chances and go back to familiarity. Orpah thought, I am going back, first chance I get. She never realized that Ruth was genuine and wanted both herself and her sis-in-law to make it, as they both were originally the outsiders. Her sister-in-law was no longer in her late teens or twenties. She did not figure she would be an outcast for having married a foreigner. She would not have the pick of the litter in choice when she got back home. Nevertheless, she had made her choice to return to where she was familiar. She feared the unknown and the struggle was hard.

Ruth had selfless qualities and that is one of the things Naomi admired about her as a daughter-in-law. I'm sure while her husband, brother-in-law, and father-in-law were alive, they all probably doted on her because she had a commanding personality. Ruth seemed to have been so very well liked that she may have been envied by Orpah, her sister-in-law, because of her likeability. Ruth felt that she married into a good family, so she trusted God and stayed with her mother-in-law.

Furthermore, I am sure her mother-in-law saw the love in her eyes when she observed how she not only tended to their family, but the way she looked at her son. That is always something pleasing to the soul of any mother. Their relationship was that of respect and Ruth knew that her mother-in-law was in charge and accepted things, as such, which made that environment that much more peaceful. Naomi observed over the course of their living together while married to her son and after her son's death that this young woman was selfless, caring, kind-hearted, and humble. These were indeed admirable attributes.

In addition, once it was just the two of them and Naomi realized that Ruth was not going back to her people and kept her company on the treacherous road back to their village, she knew that she was going to do whatever it took to make sure that this young lady is schooled in how to get a husband, while remaining respectable. By not abandoning Naomi and not placing her own needs before her mother-in-law, Ruth exhibited kindness, love, and respect for her mother-in-law. The unmentionable is that although she had been married and widowed, Ruth's reputation was intact as she was not frivolous. Naomi knew that Ruth would not leave her again and would do anything she wanted. The beauty of their relationship was that it was not manipulated, it was an understanding of what became a mother daughter relationship in their bond with one another.

Yes, sadly, I'm not going to take out the violins, but these were two women who were alone and had only each other. They were unprotected, had very little money and therefore, it was open season for folks to have taken advantage of their situation. It was a dire situation to be in. Ruth wanted to work to help her mother-in-law get by and ask Naomi if she could go and work in the fields.

There were other fields Ruth could have gleaned in, yet she felt God sent her to Boaz's location. She must have observed young men her age and had no interest. However, when she noticed the smile and excitement on Boaz's face when he stood before her, and how kind he was to her when he wrapped the wheat & barley for her to take home, Ruth reported this to her mother-in-law. Her mother-in-law was elated and devised a plan on what Ruth should do when interacting with Boaz.

Ruth was getting the evil eye from the women working in the field, who thought, oh man, she just got here and got his attention? Is she a gold digger? However, Ruth played it cool, remained focused, and was not in competition with the other women. She paid them no mind and went about her business. Ruth saw everything that she was looking for in this man and got a thumbs up from Naomi as to how to proceed with their customs. Ladies, you know, when you know. And Ruth knew! As a woman, Ruth was not going to play hard to get. She noticed the interest in his eyes when he looked at her. So, at the advice of her mother-in-law, she focused her attention on Boaz. She smiled, probably batted her eyelashes and everything.

Sometimes the heart may see what is invisible to the eye, however, Ruth saw more and there is nothing wrong with this. She did not care that he was older. Ruth knew the hidden possibilities of Boaz and pictured in her head that he was the one. But when he told her what he was about to do for them, she knew Boaz meant business. He took charge, he was ready to be the head of their family because he had proven his love for her.

Everyone is looking for someone to enhance their lives. Ruth saw herself in a home, she saw stability, and she was going to utilize her prowess to get her there. Ruth's feelings really grew towards Boaz. She knew that Boaz could give her that and more, so she summoned not only Naomi's blessing and counsel, but prayed to God for guidance, as well. She was spotted immediately by this man. These are facts, not blasphemy. Ruth's inherent features as a foreigner were what attracted him. And yes, she was different, and we can call it using her feminine wiles to get her way. Ruth was successful because he showed immediate interest without Ruth having to open herself physically. Who would not want to live a better life where everything is better, but great? Boaz was attentive and he tended to her immediate needs. Ruth was within childbearing years, she could cook, clean, make bread, heck, she was a whole bakery. Not every pie is as good as Patti Labelle's and we go chasing for that pie in the sky down that rabbit hole of the unknown, every day in search of finding Ruth or Boaz. Ruth had a sure thing. This was a good man and she had found him.

Most of us are all looking for that ideal partner. After all, a good relationship is hit or miss in the happily-ever-after love category. In my case, I missed both times. I knew what the Lord saved me from, and I was not going to question it. Once I found out and felt it in my spirit that the relationship was no longer for me, I knew to run. Ruth, however, felt it in her spirit that Boaz was a good man. And, she was right, as he was good to her and good for her. Personally, I'm waiting for my Boaz.

Initially, Ruth was thinking, he really wanted to help his relative, Naomi. Then she thought, "This man has put a lot of thought into my well-being". He made her job at gleaning easier for her. He did not want her to overexert herself. Those other young men did not care one bit. She must have felt that some people needed to stop playing games with people's emotions. She knew that Boaz was serious and of God, he cares about her reputation, and he represents security, too. Boaz was a catch! Even with the guidance of her mother-in-law, Ruth is thinking, how can she show this man that she is interested, without outwardly disrespecting herself around the masses.

I feel that Boaz was in Ruth's heart as soon as he stated, I've arranged for them not to bother you, which signified safety for her. This is thoughtful and caring. That is who and what she wanted and needed in her life. Ruth felt her life was at stake because there was another man who had first choice in marrying her and was praying it was Boaz that would win her over.

There are those people who may prefer daily fun and every weekend party life. There are some others who may want to settle down and enjoy life with a partner. When you are ready for family life, you will make sure their well-being matters and you will remain resilient through life's difficulties. No one wants someone who every time life gets hard, they want to run. One thing is for sure, Ruth did not have to do much to gain Boaz's attention. She did, however, magnetize herself to him, as he was immediately drawn to her. Ruth is honorable and wise, but she is also thinking selfishly. There is nothing wrong with that, because as a widow, she wants someone who can love her the way she needs to be loved. She didn't want to change the fact that she wanted to be a wife and a mother one day. She dreamed of the comfort and security that an older man may be able to give her. Ruth wanted to maintain her dignity. Some of the young men in the interim did not appear commitment ready. She was getting older in years and did not have much more time to waste. She didn't think it was wrong for her to want this. Ruth was also thinking long term. It could be implied that on her stressful days, Ruth knew she would be able to count not only on her mother-in-law, but could depend on Boaz, as well. She knew that she was going to be in a good and secure place in her life with this man. Ruth's testimony to women is her faithfulness. This was not her original religion but her faith in God grew insurmountably. Proverbs 24:3-4 "Through wisdom a house is built, and by understanding it is established; 4 By knowledge the rooms are filled".

When we are praying for the Lord to send us someone to love and provide for us, the question becomes, are we ready to receive them? In other words, ask yourself, am I ready for the person that God is sending me? There are over a billion questions one can ask about their readiness to pursue marriage. Of course, each person can tailor questions that are applicable to them. You have got to be sure and assertive in the statements that you make. This is what I bring; this is what I do; this is what I will do; and this is what I want in return. Remember, it's a partnership!

Today, there are so many questions that we can make a yes or no list. If we are willing to be truthful to ourselves, then by all means, let's answer some of these light questions. Am I ready to commit to one man? What can I offer him or bring to the table? How do I feel about attending counseling? Did I complete school? Am I in school? How will I react to past relationships and friendships? How do I fight and what is not acceptable and off-limits? When asked by his family and friends, what is her profession? Can I answer anything along the lines of I'm in school to be a… or I am a…! Am I willing to be monogamous? Can I carry the weight if this man becomes unemployed? Do I want to be his momma? If I become unemployed, how am I going to help in the household? Can I take constructive criticism that will benefit the relationship? Can he handle that I make more money and respect me? Can I cook a healthy meal or am I going to dial for take-out every night? Do I want children? Do I know that I'm going to love this man because he has already demonstrated he is going to love me, as well?

Listen, none of these young guys, yeah, I said it, not one, is professing or displaying a promise of commitment or even interest in Ruth. Notice I did not say long-term commitment because that's an oxymoron, as a commitment is ongoing. A commitment is a lasting promise, which means dedication, pledge, devoted or obligated to keep a promise, however long it takes.

A man enters the role of maturity as a provider, protector, and procreator. These are part of the attributes which make him who he is. He is not a moocher. Boaz placed the needs of someone he loves before his own because if she is happy and comfortable, she will in turn make him happier and at ease to be his true self. Ruth knew Boaz was committed to her by his promise to take care of this once and for all. This woman took advice, was prayerful, patient and trusted the power of God. And Boaz did not let her down. This was shown by the way he took charge in a public arena and professed to the world that he wanted her and took immediate action to prove it. To Ruth, Boaz' action demonstrated that he was going to be the head of her household, and by taking charge, he had proven his love for her on a very grand scale. Now that's commitment!

Ruth is my hero. Her work ethics in gleaning and her faith is immeasurable. Ruth was married and widowed, which to me meant she would have wanted a meaningful relationship and a family. She wanted to settle down. From the advice of Naomi, Ruth not only made a smart choice in a potential husband who was like a mayor of the town, but she guaranteed a place for herself and her mother-in-law in his heart. She made a choice to remain steadfast without knowing there was going to be a future promise that was unforeseen, who became the bloodline of the lamb that would save the world. Jesus!

Ruth was an asset, an all-around prize, and ready for Boaz to find and snag her. She was smart, she was within childbearing age and wanted children, she worked hard, she could cook, and clean, she had already experienced how to run a household and could take care of a man. She was ready! Proverbs 31:10-12 "Who can find a virtuous woman? for her price is far above rubies. 11 The heart of her husband doth safely trust in her, so that he shall have no need of spoil. 12 She will do him good and not evil all the days of her life".

Although she had a mother-in-law who wanted a better life and future for herself as well as Ruth, it was because of Ruth's obedience and her faithfulness, that God's hands were all over her. Her optimism for a promising future is a prelude of faith and the great-great-grandmother status. The power of faith brought her to produce the line to Jesus.

Boaz loved and honored Ruth. Now Ruth felt complete because she wanted a husband who would become a helpmate and father to their children. For her, there was nothing else missing. Proverbs 11:16 "A kindhearted woman gains honor".

In Search of Ruth or Boaz

* * * * * * * * * * * * * * * * * * *

Chapter VII

This Applies to…

Although our lives are changeable and our journeys vary, when it comes to matters of the heart, so many of us may share the same emotions.

Many of us do not want to feel left out of engagement parties, wedding events and desperately want to be seen with the crowd! The people around us do not make it any better, as they egg us on. Oh, Suzie Q got married, so when is it going to be your turn? Your mom, family, and other friends expect the same from you, uh? Therefore, the pressure is on you to find a partner. The anxiety of your mind and stomach start churning as the clock is ticking! Woe is me. I am by myself. I cannot find anybody. As we get older, we may become desperate to find a spouse. To say time is fleeting is an understatement. This is when it appears that everyone and everything around you seemingly becomes a matchmaker.

We want to find that ideal microwaveable partner, which means everything happens quickly because time is running out. We waste time on foolishness. However, getting to know your partner may take time. Since we are already wasting time on nonsense, why not spend time on the vetting process, too? Yes, just like interviewing and getting to know the person you are about to hire for a job. Ping! There go the tapping buttons of likes on your dating app. With each ping sound and like, you are either going to keep or discard any potential interest. The good news is that you do not have to respond to any of the requests.

Looking for a Ruth or Boaz to provide a complete course, when dating, does not necessarily have to mean dinner, a movie, then sex on the first date. Although there are a lot of married couples that this has happened to, it is, however, unlikely that sex on the first date may lead one to the altar. Your paths may never cross again, or if they do, they will be on opposite sides of the street, if you remember each other at all. They either will have lost your phone number and moved on to the next person or you may not be interested in them for whatever reason. In rare cases, they may become stalkers. This may have just been a sexual encounter or a good time for them, and there was no emotional connection made. Yep, I dare say, it was only lust. This may be what both parties wanted, and it is rare that it is a forever thing. It is not that some folks are holier than thou, but most young women from a strict, religious, or traditional family may not easily be swayed into premarital sex. This means our attempts to remain steady and grounded in the uncertainties of the unknown suitor who may blow into our lives as tempests, storms, hurricanes, or tsunamis, stand out as disrespectful.

Thus, it has been drilled into our minds that this can only be no good. In desperation due to loneliness, there are those relationships where the couple bypasses courtship period and runs right to the justice of the peace. It is after the nuptials and the honeymoon phase dissipate that you are learning who they are. There are so many issues that we miss when we do not take the time to get to know each other. Mental health often gets overlooked as a topic of discussion because no one wants to deal with it because it is a challenging subject. We cannot just pick a partner by throwing their options on a wall like wet paint, and see what sticks or say, Eeny Meeny Miny Moe, catch a piggy by the t… You get the rest, and then whoops, it's not good! Picking a mate from the bottom of the barrel in the hopes of being in the married crowd does not serve the marriage and may become a formula for disaster.

For example, when someone knows that they have given their best in a marriage and no matter how much they try, it's not good enough because their partner is just self-seeking or an infidel, they may have to decide if they want to continue pouring into a self-absorbed bottomless pit, who will never reciprocate the love given to them. One should not need permission to walk away if that is a choice. It's ok to walk away than to let them walk all over you. Affirming self-love is the key because not only does God love you, but you love yourself.

Furthermore, knowing your self-worth and value, as well as valuing your partner makes the relationship not only loving but respectable, as well. You are not going to remain that 18-year-old, nor should you remain that age when you turn 25, 30, and so forth. 1 Corinthians 13:11 "When I was a child, I spoke as a child, I understood as a child, I thought as a child; but when I became a man, I put away childish things". With maturity comes evolution and growth. Therefore, since we are maturing, this potential partner must also be more than compatible with you. They must demonstrate ethical qualities and be encouraging enough to elevate you. One side should not be doing all the work and heavy lifting. In other words, you cannot keep pouring into their cup and have a leak in yours or it's broken or damaged.

In addition, one of you cannot be the only person compromising their own needs. There needs to be a balance that serves the two, so that both parties are pouring into each other's cup. Cohesively, it simply goes hand in hand and becomes one unit. Ask yourself, am I their priority or am I an afterthought? Can we sit and have an open-ended discussion without it becoming heated with name calling expletives? How do they act when they are upset? Does an argument turn physical? Can we put the conversation on hold to be reset, fix the underlying issue then start over with therapy this time? Do they know what makes you sad and do the things that make you happy? Do they uplift you? How do they feel about therapy? Yes, therapy is a win-win, even at the dating stage, but is necessary for married couples as well.

On a different wavelength, it is said that men are from Mars and women are from Venus! Simply read, it means that folks are opposites. The question is how am I supposed to read your mind if you do not tell me what is wrong?

Conversating is a road to learning each other's nuances. Be your true self! Bring authenticity into the relationship by speaking the truth and being forthcoming. The ability to express yourself and the ins and outs of your journey will alleviate the clutter. Thoughts run wild, and communication, or lack thereof, fluctuates in the silence of a simple buzz or whisper, when it is ignored. Meanwhile one partner is on mute, thinking, he's cute, the other may not have any interest, at all. How can you get on the same page? Is there no compatibility? The matchmakers are out there and may be uncannily matching some of those who should never have been paired.

Some people are always going to have input to flatten, discourage, or break down your spirit when you do not side with their choice. However, always walk in your greatness towards who you think your life's partner should be, no matter what the doubters or the naysayers are shouting. We must communicate what our preference is and listen to each word flowing out of their spirit. Thus, we will know how genuine they are, and if it is from God. As you think about the situation, ask God for discernment and strength to help you make the right choice. Isaiah 40:31 "but those who hope in the Lord will renew their strength. They will soar on wings like eagles; they will run and not grow weary; they will walk and not faint". Be relentless in your faith in God. A believer will remain grounded in the uncertainties and will not break, no matter what storms come around them. Your joy matters in the choice you make. That is a hallelujah moment for me!

Do you still have butterflies when you see your partner? Does your face light up each time they enter a room? You know, the general good feeling that nothing else exists but the two of you and all is well with the world's good-good feeling of floating on air. You will know that this is your person. The secret is that throughout your journey whether at 5, 10, 20, 30, 40+ years later, your heart should still be pounding with the same excitement for them.

Did we close the old chapter or are we carrying past wounds as dead weight? Putting your broken pieces together before bringing someone into your space is important. Many of us have had our hearts broken; however, we must allow a healing spirit to enter our hearts before moving into any new relationship. You don't have to fake or make up stuff as you go to make yourself into something you are not. You will forget the lies and gravitate to your personal self-lenses, and eventually, they will see through your fakeness. Give yourself up-front permission to strip and unlock the hidden inner self and be the genuine you. Those who can do this wind up forming an inseparable loving bond because the two of you truly become one that nothing can come between. Nothing!

Is spirituality a part of your conversation? Does your partner pray for you? Do they pray for your union to flourish? Do you attend the same church? Do you attend church at all? If you are a praying person, how grateful are you for the blessings you have received? Discussing gratitude on a regular basis, not only at Thanksgiving, is essential to bonding and aligning the path in your journey. We are so busy wanting to experience the immediate heat of the moment which may fade that we do not know the basics. Yes, you will get butterflies, but "will you stand by me through thick and thin, will this person love me, even at times when they do not like me?" To experience true love is everything. Yeah, there are no guarantees in life. However, there is nothing wrong with confirming what will change the trajectory of your life through communicating what matters.

What happens after the relationship begins, the giggles and the smoke blowing up your ego fades, finances deplete, the bills are piling up, and our physical appearance becomes blurred, everything else that was holding the relationship snaps, cracks and pops? If it is not a good and solid relationship or if the relationship is fake, the truth will nastily come out. Relationships, just like your body, need to be nourished. Intriguing conversations and inviting your imagination to flow and commune as one with your soulmate, is a good start. You know, the one person who knows and understands you better than anyone else. They spend time, inspire, have fun, and keep the love aflame and help improve your relationship with one another.

After a break-up with a former partner, did we close that chapter, the question becomes. Did we put the lingering trust issues to bed? Are we disciplined enough to commit again? Do not confuse old longing and deception with love, because it's NOT! There is a reason why someone became an ex. There may be numerous reasons why they became "formerly known as" because something went wrong. This may have been a person who damaged your spirit, cheated, made you feel insecure, did not spend time with you, did not provide great care to you, and was abusive, while being apologetic at the same time, but you are still holding that baggage with you. Some of us carry so much baggage that our issues are deeply embedded within us, and we are traumatized. It is great to discuss any residual problems and clarify any potential issues which may have caused a breakup.

Without being too specific in today's versatile egotistical partnership, can one's insecurities and fears be stifled by the negative vibes, as even a simple question can damage or hinder a potentially great relationship? We keep the truth from one another, fearing judgment or worse, a breakup. The truth may remain hidden forever and we wonder why we cannot sleep at night. We have to deal with it! 2 Timothy 1:7 God has not given us a spirit of fear, but of power and of love and of a sound mind".

A simple question like, are you still in touch with your ex-partner? Are you only looking for a monogamous partnership? If yes, why do you allow them access to you? The question is: why are you in this relationship with me? This needs to be addressed and made known at the beginning. "Why?" Those doors need to remain closed and sealed, or else one can open them again. Let us not forget that God showed you who they were the first time. Yes, if you are ready to be with this new person, you must let the old one go.

I mean cut them off, totally! Then move forward. Comparing a new relationship with any previous one, is like being conflated with the Jones. Constant comparison will deflate the posture of how good the relationship should be. Besides, know that the grass is not always greener on the other side. However, when we do not openly deal with whatever happened before this relationship, and subsequently do not discuss it with this new person, it will creep in, and cause harm. We know that our unresolved past brings horrible triggers into our new relationship. That is why as we get comfortable with a partner, becoming vulnerable is part of our bonding process. Excuses such as, I did not mention this because I never wanted you to use it against me may result in mistrust in the relationship.

I was afraid that you would leave me. Lies and omission do not open our hearts, nor does it allow compassion towards your person. The discomfort from lying or omitting truths will place one on the edge in thoughts of, what if they find out, which may make us uncomfortable, insomniac or anxious. Morally, holding back or telling partial truths is a lie. It may be otherwise deceiving not to establish conversation or dialogue. Be forthcoming. Lying, manipulating, omitting, and falsifying facts is unbecoming of a relationship seeker. I am going to tell you a secret. Lying is bad overall.

Listen, on another note, please do not lie to a person if there's no interest or are just seeking a one-night stand. Do not go on a date if you are just looking for a free expense-paid dinner. Do not marry for immigration purposes knowing you have a girlfriend somewhere else. Do not go out and then pretend you left your wallet at home. Do not lie if you are not ready for a relationship. The more conversation and time invested in getting to know a person, the more relaxed you will become in discussing whatever your likes and dislikes warrant.

Depending on the way that the discussion evolves, this experience may indeed bring rejection, unworthiness, mistrust, confusion, and even a disconnect. However, being accountable for a loving relationship is satisfying, and in truth, each of us will know where they stand. Most importantly, questioning, are we happy? Do we know what we want? Did we pray about it? Are we getting married for the right reasons, or do we just want to leave home, and marriage is the best way out? Yes, you know, the mad rush to leave home to attempt to avoid loneliness or just getting the hell out of dodge to gain freedom, or so we think. This is not a good reason to pack and run away from home. We need to take our time and not be in a rush because we will miss out on a lot. Stay focused!

Happiness is a choice because you don't want to be miserable.

The same thing goes for not having a choice to choose your partner in life, which makes one melancholy. Why? Because you have allowed others to make the choice for you. Your input matters! Did I have an option in this crucial life-changing decision? When you make the right decision, there may be a light at the end of the tunnel. Depending on the option chosen, even if it had been the wrong choice, not because it did not turn out right, but because it was a poor choice that could have been avoided. Whatever option is chosen, a cobblestone of regrets will be acceptably smoother because it was your decision to make.

No one said to detach from the world because you are married now. It is encouraged to have a trusted small circle of friends, have dreams, and not drop everything out of your life because you are married or in a romantic relationship. It would not be fair to shut out your family and friends once you have settled down. Your spouse would find that strange and would want to be included. They may even be excited to be included in all the moments of your life. However, having someone who brings peace, and love and makes the rough road smoother is one of the greatest attributes one can provide in a relationship. To be in that oneness covenant is the ultimate find. Ding, ding, ding, screaming on the inside, I have found my person!

Once you have found your ideal mate, do not bring your best friend, their friends, your parents, or their friends into the household discussion. Do not feel you have to hang out with your single friends all the time. They will be doing 'single' outings, which does not pertain to you as a married person. Do not place yourself in awkward, precarious, or compromising situations. Sometimes the Lord must save us from ourselves. You may think that it is your sister-girl, your best buddy from band camp, or that's your fraternity brother. However, have you ever heard of envy, jealousy, haters, or someone wanting to be you, especially if things are going great with your spouse and things are not going so great for them. You and your partner are now one, and unless there is violence involved, the folks around you should know to back off. Keep your business in your house. Yes, keep your love-life private and work your issues out together.

When some of us do not get to live our own lives because we are busy worrying about other folk's feelings and opinions, we are not happy. We are worried about what someone is going to say about it, we are worried about tradition, or we would rather choose peace over our own happiness and not rock the boat. Battling other people's insecurities is rough because the equation affects us but at the same time excludes us. If you know who makes you happy, it does not matter what other people have to say. We must persevere and open the pages and chapters of our lives. In other words, write your own story. Embrace your choice. Never be afraid to reinvent yourself because complacency, stagnation and being cemented stumps growth! Give yourself some grace and reassurance that all is well with me! What is a personal choice, you ask?

Your personal choice may mean that you are satisfied that mom and dad picked out the best partner for you. It's still a choice that you have made. You jumped on the same page as them. You are the only one holding the pen when you are writing your life's story. You agreed. The choice is yours!

Being one connects us body, mind and soul. One cannot fake it 'til we make it in a marriage. It is dishonest. With all due respect, this is why open and honest communication about intimacy should not be considered taboo when communicating with your spouse. Comfortable discussions are crucial to have. Do not take each other for granted. Continue having marriage date night. Yes, dating your spouse whether you have been married for 1 or 70 years keeps the fire burning. Remind each other of what is important and meaningful in the relationship. Keep the tender hugs coming, as they are reassuring.

As vital as the subject of intimacy is, it is least discussed, as it is also considered taboo. How could something so important and a lifeline to a successful marriage be taboo, you ask? Well, folks are embarrassed, pretend, or outright lie about it. Why? Because we are afraid to have an open dialogue where we might offend or hurt the other person's feelings. And, thus we are in awe as to why the divorce rate is high. Maintaining a closed mouth, then years go by where no one says anything, will result in misery and dissatisfaction in silence. We must talk about it, otherwise, we may continue to have a high rate of cheating partners. Proverbs 10:19 "In the multitude of words sin is not lacking, but he who restrains his lips is wise".

Whether you leave your parent's home or leave your own apartment when you get married, newlyweds must realize you are getting a new roommate in a Boaz or Ruth. So, are we ready to share not only space but in your face funk, sweat, vulnerability, bad breath, quirks, bills, time, smelly feet, dingy work clothes, morning breath, intimacy, caressing or crying together, along with other life-living woes? In other words, will you love her despite her horrible karaoke singing voice, and will she love you for having two left feet on the dance floor? Is this the one and the same person we are considering, adoption, pregnancy, or raising children together, and sharing the hardship of life, jobs, love, and pain with?

Our future with someone is more than sharing a bed, it is partaking in everything together!

* * * * * * * * * * * * * * * * * *

Chapter VIII

Love is Love

Community is vital as part of family dynamics and our connection to one another. The love of family and friends allows us to come together to celebrate our lives at numerous events such as Thanksgiving, Christmas, church service and on a larger scale at birthday parties, weddings, christenings, even funerals. At many of these events, matchmaking remains prevalent. Along with matchmaking, people continue to utilize dating apps, friends, peers, and family proceed in arranging relationships, and most likely, this will not change any time soon.

At any rate, no matter who is attempting to pair you with someone of their liking, choice means deciding on your own. In other words, you have a choice to do whatever makes you happy. You may not agree with the match, but God knows that your heart will carry you to the one whom you love best. God gives us the freedom to choose, and he has the patience to wait on us. Psalms 139:7-8 "Where can I go from your spirit? Or where can I flee from your presence? 8 If I ascend into heaven, you are there; If I make my bed in hell, behold, you are there".

Indeed, the love and wisdom of our elders is weathered, but they are not worn, nor should they be dismissed. Our parents' advice is invaluable. It is in that same context, however, that young folks must be permitted to make their own mistakes, learn from their own life experiences, and realize their imperfections. Our children do not have to be reminded, I told you so, when a relationship does not work. That is showing grace and love. Just as we experienced life our own way, they will do so, their way. Most folks talk about unconditional love while carrying a boat load of conditions and that is hypocritical. Showing your children love is setting them free to live life as a married couple. Genesis 2:24 "Therefore shall a man leave his father and his mother and shall cleave unto his wife: and they shall be one flesh". This means that there is a shift in priorities and a strong commitment towards building a bond with our spouse. The covenant made in marriage is intentional and is specifically with our spouse, indicating that the relationship between husband and wife takes precedence over our relationship with our parents and any future children.

Although we are accountable for our own actions, I must admit that the plans I made for my kids did not come to pass. The love I have for my children is immeasurable and I wanted them to have the best of everything. Even though life did not turn out as I had planned for them, I knew I would not be in their lives forever; therefore, I taught them independence from an early age. Thus, they are self-sufficient as young men. They spend less and less time with me because they are grown-ups and have lives of their own. However, I still made the move to impose my wants on them. But deep in my heart, I know that they want the option to find their own Ruth. Everyone wants to be able to find their own Ruth or Boaz.

Despite our plans, we endure life's journey even though we do not know the outcome. That is faith, promise and God's love rolled into one. I know there is no right person or best match we can forge ourselves nor for others, but God, the ultimate planner, knows best. Proverbs 3:5-6 "Trust in the Lord with all your heart and lean not on your own understanding; 6 In all your ways acknowledge Him, And He will direct your paths".

I am in love with love! I feel that marriage should be an unbreakable bond between two people lasting forever, but it's not. A partnership is not supposed to be superficial. The inability to communicate should give both parties pause to reflect as it is part of the contributing factors in distance making. Are you still connected on a physical, intellectual, emotional level? Time is too precious to waste. When you realize you have your best friend in a spouse, who is also the love of your life rolled into one, time appears to stand still.

Oftentimes, we throw the word love out there without acknowledging its significance. Without love we would be like rabid animals. Love makes us feel all kinds of ways, however, not every marriage is ordained by God because people marry for selfish reasons.

Marriage is giving 100% of yourself to someone. You see, no relationship is without flaws, it requires effort and commitment. It's more than a feeling. Keep striving to make it better. To give love a chance, we need to not only be kind to the person whom we are in love with, we need to be kind to ourselves. This is part of self-love. The ripple effect of being unkind begins with each one of us. Just going through the motions in life is not a healthy process when you are unhappy and miserable. The simple fact is that dealing with issues not only provides closure, but it also provides a stepping stone to a kinder heart. Negativity appears in the form of harsh answers or an unapproachable frown. Some couples may not realize that their positive vibes of love, friendship, and passion for one another affect not only your household, but they also creep into the outliers of their lives as well.

Whether married, single, engaged, we have no control over how long a good relationship will last, but if we do not live in the present and are not intentional now, we would have missed out because of prefabricated fears of what if I had taken a chance at love, lingers. People either grow together or drift apart. Wondering prevents us from ever experiencing life with that person. Be free to love them! 1 John 4:18 "There is no fear in love; but perfect love casts out fear, because fear involves torment. But he who fears has not been made perfect in love".

If anyone is waiting around for the ideal and perfect partner to sweep them off their feet, they do not exist. However, once you feel you have met your match, trust in yourself, and your decision, and believe that others will come around with time, especially when grandchildren enter the picture. Choices led the chambers of our hearts to learn to love deeply because love is love! 1 Corinthians 13:4 "Love suffers long and is kind; love does not envy; love does not parade itself, is not puffed up".

I have analyzed love in practical situations and know that I have been repetitive in helping us find and perhaps maintain our partnership with Ruth or Boaz. Nonetheless, I admire Elizabeth Barrett Browning's Sonnet, "How do I love thee? Let me count the ways." She reminds me there are so many ways to nurture love. Ask yourself, am I ready for a lifetime commitment? I am not only referring to love, commitment, and the marriage registrar, which will officially record that this is a union in the State in which you live; I am referring to honoring your vows and remaining committed. Are you ready to grow at different speeds and still be able to meet somewhere in the middle? Getting married is easy. It is the divorce that may run your expenses into the thousands. When you marry, you are no longer just worrying about yourself, there is a compromising element that's involved as you are taking a spouse along with you on our journey.

How do you welcome your spouse when they come home? Do you notice when your partner is stressed? When you feel unseen and the outside world has beaten you down, your home should be an oasis.

Therefore, when you enter your home, you need a partner who will say, how was your day? A partnership is a joint effort. II Corinthians 6:14 "Do not be unequally yoked together with unbelievers. For what fellowship has righteousness with lawlessness? And what communion has light with darkness?"

In a world filled with narcissists, takers, and users, finding someone who will truly love and be there for you mentally, emotionally, financially, and physically, may be incredibly rare. While online platforms and apps attempt to match personal preferences and personalities, there may not be any pre-programmed robots that can do this perfectly. I must say that I know a few people who met online and are successfully married. The possibilities are there, so do your due diligence. We need to invest time in getting to know someone before we take the plunge. Avoid regrets, do not be a fool for a fool.

What is Regret? We sometimes say or do things we regret later. Regret may be a missed opportunity. While reminiscing we may imagine how we would have married that guy our parents introduced to us; perhaps life would have turned out differently. I'm glad I ran away and married the love of my life. I'm happy because I chose to never get married. I'm happily divorced and single once again, I should have followed my instincts. When that choice is ours to make and we do so, the if only I had, and what if I had, will not linger and gnaw at us for an eternity. When you throw the negatives out the window, and don't ask for permission, then there will be no regrets.

Stephen Stills' lyrics stated, "...If you can't be with the one you love, honey, love the one you're with…". However, your flex is to have boundaries set up so that your options are clear for you. Love the one you love!

In the solitude of my room, I have come to realize that certain choices have helped me reduce some of the sources of my stress. I made the choice in prioritizing my peace of mind which I was able to attain through forgiving someone who has wronged me. By doing so years ago, through self-love, this impacted and improved my wellbeing. I was able to not only repair certain issues, I was also able to disconnect and break free. I did not allow any revolving doors, sweet talk that it will never happen again, bring me back to something that would be detrimental to my health. I got over this dark period in my life and thank God for His love for helping me. Again, no coercion, but prayer, a pastor, counseling, or life coaches may get us to the point of forgiveness so that we may freely move forward.

A personal prayer for me is to ask God to forgive me for my preconceived thoughts of matchmaking. Lord, let us wait on your time and not remain selfish in our ways. Help us to believe you do not say no, but something else, something even better. Ephesians 3:20 "Now to Him who can do exceedingly abundantly above all that we ask or think, according to the power that works in us, 21 to Him be glory in the church by Christ Jesus to all generations, forever and ever. Amen".

When we are meddling, there comes a point when we must realize that God does not need our help. Although my mother meant well when she felt that I needed to be married to secure a better future for me, I have come to understand that I cannot superimpose my wishes and dreams of matchmaking on my children. Parents feel proud and at times unapologetic for attempting to match us with whom they believe is the perfect partner. Even though some parents may want the best for us, since we are the affected person, a discussion must be had on what we want.

One of the things to have changed my mind on matchmaking is when I received a message from a young lady whom I approached to have bible study with my son. Her words were, and I am paraphrasing, "The Holy Spirit does not need your help in bringing your son to God". I received that message with open arms and stopped attempting my matchmaking schemes immediately because I knew in my spirit that God is in control. This decision took me back to Ruth again. Although I admired Ruth and her diligence in helping her mother-in-law, I think I was biased for myself in that I wanted a good woman like Ruth in my life as a daughter-in-law. Secretly, I knew that she would take care of me in my old age, and I probably wouldn't wind up at the old age home. Reminiscent of what my momma talked about all those decades ago, I feel that I have come full circle.

Selfishly, I also wanted someone like Ruth who would love my son, and everything attached to him. Furthermore, I loved Ruth's obedience because it is the power of her faith which brought her to produce the line to Jesus. The religion she married into healed her body and soul. Her faith was so strong, that it carried her, even catapulted her to find peace and love. In that same manner, I had to be obedient and listen to the Holy Spirit telling me, I am the one who is tasked to lead, teach and guide. I, too, have obeyed, I am praying and waiting for His blessings. Matthew 7:7-8 7 "Ask, and it will be given to you; seek, and you will find; knock, and it will be opened to you. 8 For everyone who asks receives, and he who seeks finds, and to him who knocks it will be opened".

Agreeing to matchmaking is still an option that you may have chosen because you grew to fall in love with the match given to you. If you accept it, and it is not forced upon you, marriage may turn out to be the best thing for you. Allow your voice to be heard, and do not get lost in the background. Just like a friend of mine whose parents had matched her with her husband 18 years ago, they now finish each other's thoughts and sentences and are more compatible with each other than many others. To me, this makes them one. This friend of mine chose her match, so love who you love!

Whether it is a blind date from an app, your parents' match, or from the first glance meeting from across the room, I believe there is a baseline introduction. On your initial date, take a picture of the two of you. By date three or four there may be a transformational change in a wider smile in your picture because of the interest in the anticipated I can't wait to see them, daydreaming about them, or initiating follow-up calls by saying, I really like you and would like to see you again. As you notice that smile getting broader, and you continue to see each other, the transformation into dating, then courting may begin.

You never know where this may lead. It may be a start towards the rest of your life together leading to the altar. No labels, it's the start of something beautiful, called love!

* * * * * * * * * * * * * * *

EPILOGUE

Millions of us are in search of a life partner. This may take months, sometimes years before this happens. If this does not happen soon enough, continue to live your best life and be happy. Sometimes, this may not happen at all. Ask yourself, would I rather be single or put up with being with someone ratchet who annoys the heck out of me? Perhaps, I could do bad all by myself. The ideal partnership cannot be one-sided. A marriage can only be done with compromise because it takes two to want it!

As we attempt to slow down the fast-paced world around us, we may notice that life is a journey, not a competition. Although some people may attempt to redirect or misdirect our lives, we have the final say in the decision-making process. We oversee the direction we want our lives to take, however, we are not here to impose our mindset onto others, nor accept theirs onto us. Respecting each other's boundaries allows us the ability to limit access to us. Therefore, maintain full control of the decision-making of your life! Romans 12: "And do not be conformed to this world, but be transformed by the renewing of your mind, that you may prove what is that good and acceptable and perfect will of God".

Although there should be respect for young adults, there also should be boundaries that afford them the freedom to be at ease. Whether through matchmaking, dating apps or however your humble beginning of dating begins, embrace the relationship of your choice. There should be no bad feeling, guilting, or shaming your adult children for living life their way and at their own pace. There will probably be so many outliers of what other people think you should do.

Personally, I do not want to have a negative impact on anyone. The lesson I have learned from wanting to influence my will on my children is that I should let them choose for themselves. After you take a shot at making your choice, and know who you want to be with, take a deep breath and smile on the inside. Since this will be one of the most important decisions of your life, you should be picky because a soulmate is for a lifetime. Once you have thoroughly thought this through, the decision belongs to only the two parties involved.

I love my children and want the blessings of God on them. Therefore, I can pray for these adults to get closer to God, pray for their happiness and subsequent family life, then leave it at that. The rest is up to them and our father, God.

I cannot emphasize enough that the choices you make in life are all up to you! It is up to you to live the life you want! I have made my life choices with two failed marriages which ended in divorce. But I have moved on, and folks have attempted to matchmake me, again. What do I say to that? No thank you! Whatever is meant to be, will be, but when I meet Mr. Right, it will be my choice. Does that mean I will marry once again? Not necessarily, but I know that I have a choice and numerous options if I do!

I'm looking for that forever bond with my person. I believe that God walks with us through every step of our journey because He loves us. And, I will make this personal to me. Someday, when God gifts me the love of my life, I, too, will rejoice like Ruth. To me, the perfect time in life is the crossroads when you first meet and know this is your person. Not only that, but I will probably never get a second chance to make a first impression with him. I will pray that when that happens, we become inseparable. I will also pray and ask that even after years of loving each other until death do us part, and after one of us passes away, I pray when it is my time, we will reunite and sing with the angels with him. Yes, I believe that kind of life-long love still exists!

I am not a relationship expert, but I have learned a thing or two in my lifetime. Nothing changes if nothing changes, therefore, the only thing that resonates is choosing to be with whoever makes you happy!

If you haven't already found your person, go find your Ruth or Boaz! Maybe even pop the question, too.

Live and let live!

* * * * * * * * * * *

ABOUT THE AUTHOR

Ms. Thomas is a woman who loves the Lord. She is a mother, a grandmother, a registered nurse, an author and so much more. Born in Port-au-Prince, Haiti.

Ms. Thomas grew up in Brooklyn where she attended primary school in the heart of Crown Heights. Ms. Thomas later worked in Manhattan's Wall Street district for close to 20 years.

Her journey in nursing and subsequent goal towards earning a master's degree came later in life.

Ms. Thomas loves to write and dance, and her hobbies are reading, crossword puzzles, traveling, Sudoku, gardening, content creating and Zumba.

She currently lives in Florida.

* * * * * * * * * * * * * * * * * *

Look for author sue thomas on most media platforms.

↠↠↠↠↠↠↞↞↞↞↞↞

I aspire to inspire!

↠↠↠↠↠↠↞↞↞↞↞↞↞

www.ingramcontent.com/pod-product-compliance
Lightning Source LLC
Chambersburg PA
CBHW070115070426
42448CB00039B/2832
9798985836226